Go Suck A Lemon
strategies for improving your emotional intelligence

Michael Cornwall, PhD, LPCC, CSW

ISBN-13: 978-1456515607

ISBN-10: 1456515608

Please visit http://www.eitheory.com to enhance your reading experience.

For Al and Me!

Albert Ellis (September 27, 1913 – July 24, 2007) was an American psychologist who in 1955 developed rational emotive behavior therapy (REBT). He held M.A. and Ph.D. degrees in clinical psychology from Columbia University and was a member of the American Board of Professional Psychology (ABPP). He founded and was the president emeritus of the New York City-based Albert Ellis Institute. He is generally considered to be the originators of the cognitive revolutionary paradigm shift in psychotherapy and the founder of cognitive-behavioral therapies. Based on a 1982 professional survey of U.S. and Canadian psychologists, he was considered the second most influential psychotherapist in history (Carl Rogers ranked first in the survey; Sigmund Freud was ranked third). Prior to his death, *Psychology Today* described him as the *greatest living psychologist*.

PERSONAL REFLECTION DISCLAIMER

My primary obligation is to respect the integrity and promote the welfare of all individuals, families and groups. When discussing particular individuals and my experiences with them, I must take precautions to protect them from any harm resulting from that discussion. Unless agreed upon by a party, I have taken every precaution to disguise the identity of the individuals discussed in this manuscript. Any data derived from a client relationship and used in this manuscript has been disguised so that that the informed client's identity is fully protected. Any data which could not or was not disguised was authorized by the individual's informed and un-coerced consent. No notes, test data, correspondence, audio or visual tape recordings, electronic data storage or other documents were used to recollect any of the data related herein.

Table of Contents

INTRODUCTION

I am hyperaware.

People are forever telling me I should stop analyzing everyone and everything and just relax: *You think too much. You shouldn't think so much. Relax, will you!*

I am often left thinking what one would do instead of thinking.

Is there such a state of mind as not-thinking?

Coma perhaps?

I spend a lot of time thinking about that.

Growing up, emotion was not something that was celebrated in my home. The more my family avoided emotion, the more unavoidable emotion became. I learned early in my life that emotion was a sign of weakness, foolishness; like showing your cards before the end of a hand of poker: *Where's your poker face? Stay calm. Don't let 'em see you sweat.*

My family viewed emotion as a form of manipulation. Crying meant giving up. With the exception of stubbornness, anger and criticism, there was very little touching, kissing, embracing or spontaneous emotive behavior. For me, growing up was like walking an angry Chihuahua on a very short, heavy leash.

My father expected perfection.

He was often left disappointed.

Being human interfered with that objective.

****

As a child I became somewhat of a sponge, learning from experience, emoting vicariously by provoking others to react to me – burping loudly in the lunchroom, eating chalk, throwing burrs onto woolen hats, clowning and teasing. These were my emotional conduits. I discovered that people could be set ablaze with emotional color, particularly when aroused through conflict or struggle.

At the doctor's office, I watched as the other children (my sister in particular), waited for their vaccinations. *Bee stings*, the injections were called, had a different effect on each child. Some were stunned with fear; crying and pleading. Some bargained; some implored. Some played with toys, while others slept. My sister always sat and stared at the examining room door, waiting for the nurse to stick out her head and shout: *Sandra! Is Sandra here?* When her name was called, my sister bolted upright, eyes bulging from her head, frozen with fear.

Same situation, entirely different reaction.

I found all of this variation in emotion amazing, even at that young age.

(To this day I cannot imagine why anyone would tell a child something felt only like a *bee sting*, in order to calm them before an injection. As if that similarity would somehow help reduce or even eliminate a child's anxiety.)

I remember the *House of Horrors* at Nantasket Beach.

Come on, it will be fun.

I looked up in terror at the clown's big, plastic left eye hanging over its laughing rouged cheek, bobbing back and forth, keeping time with its pink, slick tongue.

I don't wanna.

I noticed very keenly how boys my same age went inside, not even hesitating, grinning at me as they ran up and into the dark black hole that served as the clown's mouth.

Baby.

And, of course, there was baseball.

By no stretch of the imagination should I have ever been allowed to play anything involving a ball. I was so near-sighted I couldn't distinguish a ball that was landing on my head from one a mile above my head. Each time I took my turn at bat, confident that I would never hit the ball anyway, the Killian brothers sat on the bench and, as if synchronized, put their arms over each other's shoulders and began to cry.

My father watched from the stands.

The team on the field sat on the ground, smiling, waiting for me to strike out.

They heard about me.

I did hit the ball once (or maybe the ball hit my bat); but instead of excitement, I remember feeling fear and expressing confusion. I froze in place, ran from home to third base (which had less to do with my poor eyesight and more to do with my level of interest in the rules of the game), while the Killians matched expressions of terror.

And the ball soared into the outfield.

How is it that each of us can be presented with the very same stimuli and concoct so many different expectations, so many varying reactions?

Incredible.

****

I spent a good part of my early life studying the phenomenon of emotion. When I entered college, I was introduced to a system of mental health designed not to make people happy but, instead, to increase *emotional intelligence*, all achieved through *better thinking*. At the time, I knew that everyone expressed any number of emotions – even in the presence of the same or similar stimuli. I didn't know that the thing that caused that difference was variations in thinking and perceiving.

Thinking was the key. *Thinking* regulated emotion.

Emotion is thought!

Thought is emotion!

If I think *differently*, I can feel *differently*.

This *emotional intelligence* idea relied upon helping people hear their own *self talk* – hear what they say to themselves just before they choose an emotional response.

Choose an emotional response?

I was so moved by this new idea, I attended a conference in Chicago organized to teach this *emotional thinking* technique. While I waited for everyone to get seated and everything to get started, I remember hearing a commotion in the back of the room.

It's him.

Look, it's him.

That isn't him.

Yes it is!

I turned to see a small, very thin and frail man heading up the aisle, carrying a can of juice and a cookie. He didn't really say nor do anything unusual. But everything about him provoked an emotional reaction. Grumpiness wafted after him like dust. He grinned, but his grin was somewhat sinister, boyish. His long nose and horn rimmed glasses made him look unapproachable, yet he shook hands with those who reached out to welcome him, showing a certain measure of enthusiasm and caring. The man may have passed for a janitor, the guy who adjusts the audio equipment, or the president of some small, impoverished eastern European nation. He was no one and everyone, all at the same time. His clothing was disheveled and he was hunched over, as if carrying a huge bundle of kindling in a bunch on his back. He ascended the single step to the stage, carefully shuffled across to his seat and sat down in front of the assembled audience. He paused for a moment, squinting through his glasses at everyone in attendance, as if looking painfully into the sun. He tapped the microphone, pushed his glasses up closer to his eyes, leaned to one side and farted!

How dreadful!

This man was going to teach me about emotional intelligence? What kind of crackpot was this?

He continued squinting over his glasses, while inspecting the microphone and looking out over his audience. In his nasally New York accent, he groused, *if I have a seizure, someone come up and feed me this juice.*

It was 1992.

His name was Albert Ellis.

EMOTIONAL INTELLIGENCE

There are those who claim that the best indicator of higher-order intelligence is through the expression of *art*, while there is growing support for the inclusion of *athletic ability* in our consideration of aptitude. And then there are those who would judge intelligence using factors such as *nature, music, numbers* and *reasoning*. Apparently, one can be *people smart, body smart, word smart, self smart, nature smart, animal smart* and *picture smart*. (No one is yet talking about *sexual performance aptitude*, as far as I know.)

The word *intelligence* is frequently used to describe school performance, the capacity to comprehend or to profit from classroom experiences. This type of intelligence is believed (in the absence of disease or trauma) to be fixed, stable, unchanging over a lifetime.

Some believe we are born with all the intellectual potential we will ever possess. There is, however, increasing discussion over the role *desire* and *tenacity* have on improving intellectual competence. Can we increase our intelligence through diligence and hard work?

Alas, because intelligence seems to be an arbitrary concept, made up of a number of unstable, evolving factors and ideas, most definitions of intelligence seem, ultimately, to alienate someone.

I attribute our passion for evolving the definition of intelligence with the ever-confounding variable: *self-esteem*. Is intelligence related, somehow, to the concept of self-esteem? Is it possible to possess good self-esteem without first measuring oneself and one's aptitude for learning as intellectually gifted? Is it possible to be of average (or less than average) intelligence and still maintain a high value of oneself?

Because intelligence appears to play such an important role in our personal assessment of ourselves, we continue to fine tune, rework and manipulate the meaning of intelligence, increasing its parameters and boundaries, improving the odds that everyone will, some day, be able to claim their unique place among our ever-growing population of geniuses.

***

Like general intelligence, *emotional intelligence* is a mishmash of theories, concepts and ideas, even more elusive than the definition of *general intelligence* (or even *self esteem*).

The good thing about emotional intelligence is, unlike general intelligence, there is widespread belief that *it is something that is likely within our control.* It may be an adaptive mechanism. We may actually be born with immense potentials for adjusting, fiddling with and modulating our emotional range in order to ensure that we can cooperate and collaborate with one another in order to survive as species. After all, we have to *get along, protect ourselves and others from predators and to mate.* To make certain that we can achieve all of these basic goals, we have to be able to *adjust* our personalities and accommodate ANY culture or subculture in which we encounter our own species.

***

Emotional intelligence is believed to be a *self-perceived* measure, far more flexible and far more under our own control than general intelligence. If you find that you're losing friends, jobs and family members, a decision to do something else, to explore other emotional options, is very much in the realm of possibilities. *Desire, effort* and *tenacity* actually CAN play a role in improving emotional intelligence.

****

The fabric of your emotional life is an elaborate quilting of experiences. From the time of your birth, each square, each life experience, is stitched to the next to create the individual you are today. A keen awareness of your genetics and how your parents, relatives, friends and neighbors solved their own emotional issues, however successful, will often provide insight into the fabric from which your emotional intelligence is woven. How do you make judgments about the obstacles you face in your life? How do you overcome them? Each time you settle an emotional issue, are you choosing the quickest and most familiar option? Or do you put some effort into choosing from your emotional range?

You've built your current level of emotional intelligence through a series of personal observations, trials and errors, punishments and rewards. And each time you apply your unique emotional resolution to the same or similar emotional event, you *add strength to it*. The more you repeat your current behaviors, the stronger and more predictable they become. Doing away with harmful behaviors often takes the strength of a wrecking ball. Improving your emotional intelligence is time consuming and often difficult. The good news is: *You can do it!*

It will take the force of will, but you can do it.

***

You may be surprised to find that many of the emotional responses you now use, although socially acceptable, are really quite dysfunctional: *That's how everyone acts when that happens. It's natural to be angry if someone says that to you.* In addition to accepting the inevitability of your conditioned emotional response, your use of *exaggeration, oversimplification, overgeneralization, illogic, unproven assumptions, faulty deductions* and *absolutistic notions* are all believed to be detrimental to the process of improving emotional intelligence. Many of your emotional responses, regardless of how much strength you've given them, can be brought down, deconstructed and reshaped. You will just have to learn how to give your knee-jerk response to emotional stimuli less strength – LESS OF A JERK. To do that you will have to commit to reinventing the way you think and behave.

- You will approach that task by accepting and then adapting to a no-nonsense style of emotional problem solving.

- You will learn and use a process of level-headed decision-making.

- You will try to become more efficient, flexible and open-minded when addressing your emotional problems.

- You will learn that there is always another emotional option.

- You will learn to make fact-based observations, something most of us are unfamiliar with doing.

- You will also incorporate *in vivo* (in life) exposure, i.e., homework, to encourage you to independently act against your learned thoughts and behaviors.

In the end, after reading this book, you will become more informed, increasingly more capable and far more emotionally *self-reliant*. Instead of being your own worst enemy, you will become your own best friend – your own therapist.

We may be strengthened when we learn to be emotionally self-reliant, to free ourselves from emotional helplessness and our dependence on others for our emotional solutions.

It will take the force of will to do that.

STRATEGY ONE

Emotion is an inner language

Remember the feeling you had when you were first exposed to a foreign language?

Bonjour classe! Comment allez-vous aujourd'hui?

My first day of high school French was like being kicked in the throat with a Louis Vuitton.

D'accord. On y va!

French was an indecipherable code; a landscape of rolling Rs. The language was simply noise to me. My first reaction to the French language was to protect myself from it. To stay happily within my American English comfort zone.

I was taught through *emersion* – being dipped in French, so to speak. I was expected to speak French all the time. When the odd occasion arose, and I was allowed to speak English, I was noticeably relieved, as if being released from confinement.

"Do you have any questions," my French *professeur* would ask, after meeting with me concerning my failing grade.

"No," I said.

"Voila! C'est finis!"

I could feel the hand of the *Language of Love* reach over and cover my mouth, "But I'm not finished!"

"En Français," she would immediately say, "Maintenant, en Français."

"Ummmmmmm . . . J'ai besoin de plus de temps. J'ai beaucoup plus pour parler!"

"Très bon! Mais je n'ai plus le temps. Nous pouvons parler demain. OK?"

"D'accord . . . but I don't like it."

"En Français!"

***

For many of us, language brings comfort and provides safety. Language can be used to lash out at our enemies and to woo our lovers. Language can initiate war and negotiate peace. French did not offer me comfort or safety. It provided confusion. I couldn't convey my emotions or express my desires without frustration.

Prior to learning to speak French (and I eventually did), I took language entirely for granted. Language, over night, became a source of considerable frustration. I couldn't beg for a better grade, go to the boys' room, sharpen my pencil or explain my tardiness without first laboring through the rules of language. The further the French language tried to drag me away from my native tongue, the tighter I clung to the pillar of English.

Non! Si vous plait! Je ne peux le faire plus!

French was a challenge not only to my intellectual development, but it also impacted my social and personal growth. Trying to maintain my status as a gloomy, sullen teenager, while speaking French, was out of the question. It meant making mistakes; being ridiculed. I was being graded on my willingness to stand and, through trial and error, systematically make a fool of myself. All of this at a time when self-consciousness and insecurity was the central force in my evolving development. I made no attempt to use an accent or show any level of enthusiasm. I slouched and pronounced every consonant in exactly the same way it would be pronounced by a rebellious, English-speaking young man with a troubled future.

It takes time, dedication and a certain amount of devotion to practice a new language. It also takes passion, something I intentionally removed early (but made up for later on) from my French education. I didn't want to learn to speak French. I was happy speaking English. Everyone I knew spoke English. (Except Jacque Cousteau – but at least he tried.) I knew my way around English. It fit. And it didn't hurt every time I wanted to say something. The language of emotion can present many of the same challenges.

***

Emotion is an *inner language*, the language of the mind, learned through exposure, shaped by thought and expressed through behavior. Your current emotional language, the language found in your *self-talk* (the things you say to yourself about what is happening to and around you), is the language you are most comfortable using.

Self-talk, the way you talk to yourself, greatly impacts your emotional life.

Each of us tends to use our own inner language, with limited variability, to determine how we will *think* and *feel* about anything , from the death of a loved one, to lying, being ridiculed, stealing, being in love, getting a failing grade, cheating and social injustice. And we have emotional expectations of each other, because most of us speak a similar emotional language.

> *She was rude to me.*
> *Well, that was horrible.*
> *Yes, it was horrible.*
> *I would be so pissed.*
> *I am pissed.*
> *That can be expected.*

The similarities between learning to speak a foreign language and learning to hear and then change your *inner language* will become clearer as you progress through this learning adventure. Suffice it to say, you will meet the same language barriers I described above when you *try to change your inner language and replace it with something new.* It will all seem very foreign, but it will eventually make sense.

> *She was really to me.*
> *Well, that was horrible.*
> *It wasn't really all that horrible.*
> *I would be pissed.*
> *I am feeling a bit frustrated, but that will pass soon.*
> *I don't know how you can do that.*

There is no doubt, after learning your new language you will want to revert back to your old way of talking to yourself. If you stick with it, however, the task of changing your self-talk will become less burdensome. Your lingering challenge will be living in a world where everyone you meet will want you to speak your old inner language.

That particular argument will never end.

For instance, you are in a convenience store and the cashier talks on her cell phone while she completes her transaction with you. She doesn't acknowledge you. Your inner language may be, "She *should* care about me. She *should* not be rude to me. She *should* appreciate my patronage." After having this inner discussion with yourself, you may find yourself expressing some form of anger.

Why?

Well, because you are telling yourself (your self-talk) that people *should* behave according to your personal rules and regulations. The cashier is obviously not interested in following your rules and you think she *should* change her behavior and follow your orders. Through self-talk, you may justify some sort of retort or action to compel the woman into compliance with your expectations of her behavior. Improvement in your emotional intelligence, however, will be achieved when you begin to tell yourself (your self-talk), instead, that people have *a perfect right to behave unprofessionally* and *unfriendly* because they have a perfect right to make poor choices with their social behavior.

(I know; this is a tough one; but they do.)

If you think about it, people have every right to behave any way they choose to behave, rightly or wrongly – goodly or badly. You behave the way you choose; why can't anyone else?

Improvement in emotional intelligence might be realized when our self-talk includes such rational reasoning as, "Her behavior is unusual. She isn't choosing to be very friendly, which is her right to choose. I don't *need* her to be friendly in order to complete this transaction. It would be nicer, but I don't *need* it. I don't think it's a good thing for her to choose this way of interacting with customers, but she can choose to make poor choices, and I can still be happy in my own life."

***

Your thoughts are your inner emotional language.

Your emotional language dictates how you make interpretations of behavior, your own and other's. Your interpretation is often decidedly skewed on the side of *selfishness*. You believe that because you want someone to behave a certain generally accepted way, it must be that way, regardless of what the other person might think. The fact of the matter is there is a point at which your emotional life ends and where another's emotional life begins. It might be best to recognize and appreciate that distinction.

Your emotional language, your self-talk, ordains your emotional reaction. We often mistake our own rules as law, truth and fact when, in reality, they are simply our preference turned into demands and needs.

People should not treat me with disrespect.

Why?

I don't like it.

Should people behave according to your likes or their own?

Mine.

What happens when they don't?

They should be punished.

***

You are capable of expressing boundless emotion, nearly all of which is intentional and nearly all of it drawn from creative thinking (self-talk). There is nothing natural about fearing *failure*, for example. Likewise, there is no evidence for feeling *guilt* when you make a mistake. But if you craft your emotional language in such a way as to make *failure* and *guilt* your only emotional options, they will likely be your only options. For example, if you were raised in an environment filled with expectations of *perfection*, you might avoid new experiences because new experiences require some level of *risk-taking*. Risk-taking increases the possibility of *failure*. Your emotional language might guide you to equate failure with evidence of your *worthlessness: If I fail at something it can only mean one thing: I am a failure.* Who would take a risk if failure meant being labeled useless and worthless? On the other hand, if you were encouraged as a child to try new things and not to be overly concerned if things don't go as planned, you might think differently: *If I fail at something it means I have learned from the experience and could do better next time I try it*. If you change your emotional language, you will change your emotional response to nearly anything. That process takes time, dedication and a certain amount of devotion to practicing a new language – new self-talk.

It also takes passion to change.

When I started challenging my own inner language, I often wanted to give up, to return to what I already knew. I wasn't always as happy as I could have been, but at least I knew my way around my old self talk. And it didn't hurt every time I wanted to think or say something. Just like giving up your native tongue, you will cling to your learned emotional language, your self-talk, because you know it so well. You rely on your self-talk to help you through life. Your self-talk is comfortable, and you will hold on to it until you are convinced that the benefit of changing it outweighs the benefit of maintaining it.

You can feel something else other than anger.

Oh, really? What else can I feel?

You could feel sadness.

I don't want to feel sad. I want to be angry.

That's your choice.

Yes, it is.

You don't often have a choice in how others react to you. You almost *always* have a choice in how you react to others. As you progress through this text, you will be challenged to learn a new emotional language, a new way of talking to yourself.

It will take the force of will to use it.

STRATEGY TWO

Strengthening your emotional resolve

There are a few topics I would like to emphasize early in our discussion –

Absolute Terms: Improving your emotional intelligence will depend on your application of the very best definition of the words *should, ought, must, have to* and *need*. These words are referred to as *absolutes* and leave little room for mistake or free will. For example, *People should treat me with respect. He should behave better than that. I need your cooperation to be happy in my life. You ought to behave according to the accepted rules. You SHOULD, OUGHT, MUST, HAVE TO and NEED to behave perfectly. If you don't, I cannot be happy until you do.*

I often find students are very ambiguous about the *implied* meaning of *should, ought, must, have to* and *need*. Without an exceptional, *operational definition* of what these words truly mean, this process of improving your emotional intelligence can become meandering and meaningless. I encourage my reader to be very familiar with how s/he uses these terms and how they have a great deal of potential to interfere with improving our self-talk. Essentially, when you use these words, if you think people *should, ought, must, have to* and *need* to behave according to *your* wishes, or some accepted standard, you will often be let down.

People behave according to their own rules.

Confusion often arises over the danger of using the words *should, ought, must, have to* and *need*, because these are words often used in our culture to express an *ideal*: *People should be kind to one another*, is the expression of an ideal. *People should not lie or steal*, is yet another standard of excellence. These are models of behavior that most of us respect. They are, however, not laws and they certainly are not how everyone chooses to behave at all times. When you use these words, you are declaring your preference for perfection and your intolerance of variation. No one, including you, can live their entire lives in an ideal state. Make A LOT of room for imperfection in your life and in the lives of others and your emotional intelligence will grow by leaps and bounds.

You should not behave that way and I can't stand it when you do can become *I would prefer that you behave differently and I can stand it when you're not perfect*.

I need you to be my friend and I will suffer until you are can become *I would like you to be my friend, but I can live my life well enough if you're not*.

Using words like *should, ought, must, have to* and *need* not only take away the fallibility of being human, but they deny the fact that others often make unintentional mistakes or simply exercise their free will to behave any way they choose. So, if you would like to make an immediate improvement to your emotional intelligence, you may begin by paying close attention to your use of these words and begin to replace them with some variation of the terms WANT or WOULD LIKE; words that make your preference of others more flexible.

***

I once had a client who simply could not bend her belief to any measureable degree in how people *should* always behave and how she *needed* people to behave in order for her to be happy in her life. She set her mind on the idea that there were standards of behavior that everyone *should, ought, must, have to* meet, and people *should, ought, must, have to* be condemned if they did not abide by her definition of how people *should, ought, must, have to* behave. Her over-emphasis on these words may have been responsible for her starting therapy. The world was jam-packed with people breaking all the rules. As you can imagine, her life was in a perpetual state of let down.

As is the custom with younger people these days, she was covered in tattoos. She had tattoos on her neck, her legs, her arms and on her shaved head. I thought it might be best to use those particular personal choices to better illustrate the true meaning of *should, ought, must, have to* and *need*.

"But isn't getting a tattoo sort of a male ritual?" I asked.

She looked at me suspiciously, "What on earth are you talking about?"

"You have several tattoos on your legs and arms. Isn't that something only boys *should* do? Girls *shouldn't* do that."

"Girls can do whatever they want these days. This is the twenty first century, for God's sake."

"That may be, but when I was growing up, girls didn't get tattoos."

"OK, what do you want me to do about it?"

"Well, I believe you *shouldn't have any tattoos.*"

"You're wrong. I can do whatever I want to myself."

"My beliefs are valid and yours are not," I said, leaning forward. "You should behave according to my rules and standards. I need your cooperation. I cannot be as happy as I NEED to be in my life without your cooperation. I'm in charge of the world and you should follow my rules."

"I'm not changing my beliefs."

"Exactly."

When you use the words *should, ought, must, have to* and *need*, pay attention to the idea that you are declaring that anyone who interacts with you must meet the ideal standard that YOU set, TO THE LETTER; and that your continued happiness depends on the world operating to the letter of your ideal standard.

***

Honorable Beliefs: Beliefs, which will take up a majority of our discussion, can almost always be made healthier, rather than entirely abandoned. I often find students saying they are happy with their beliefs, because they are good beliefs to hold: *Other people should change their beliefs, instead. Mine are fine the way they are.* Beliefs about politeness, courtesy, respect, the law and patience seem to be the main beliefs people want to hold on to. For example, your belief in mutual respect is an *honorable belief*. The fact is, although your belief is something that is intended to uphold a worthy standard, or is a belief that is commonly held, your beliefs are not consistently held by everyone – not even you.

Preserve your honorable beliefs!

They are the standards we will use one day to judge the merits of our culture. But, in the meantime, in order to increase your emotional intelligence, you will have to modify your strictly held beliefs so that they recognize the reality that some people will not accept your beliefs – no matter how much you think they *should*. You might say, instead, "I like it when people treat each other with respect, but when they don't, I can still live with it," rather than being angry and demanding that people immediately change their behavior to meet your expectations. "I can be sad that people are disrespectful. I will never like it, but I can remain content when it happens. I can treat others with respect, regardless of the way people choose to behave toward me. It will be hard to do, but so is improving my emotional intelligence." You are not being instructed to change any of your beliefs to include behaving badly. You are being invited, however, to accept that sometimes your beliefs are not held at all times by everyone around you.

Prepare for that.

Instead of expressing anger, which is often the result of not getting what you think you should have or that you think you need, you can, instead, feel sadness, forgiveness, unhappiness in the face of not getting what you would *prefer*.

***

Being an Advocate for Change: Emotional intelligence is not improved by becoming a passive observer of the world's failures. Passive acceptance of poor behavior is not how most people often encounter adversity. Being in the frame of mind to help and teach (a flexible, forgiving and pardoning frame of mind), rather than one meant to annihilate and destroy, will make your request for better behavior choices more likely to be heard and appreciated by others.

You are being rude.

Yeah?

You are calling me names and pointing at me.

So?

Although I like you generally, if you continue to treat me this way, I will forgive you for your poor choices, but I won't speak with you any further. I will also be hesitant to ask for your input in the future.

Hmmmmmm.

Emotional intelligence is best improved by perceiving
interpreting your *external reality* and making more functional, inte
judgments by changing your perception and interpreting differently.
ideas, your beliefs and your demands are not imperatives to anyone but
you. (Even you don't always live up to the demands have of others.) It is
true that your beliefs (your *shoulds, oughts, musts, have tos* and *needs*) are likely
beliefs that, if shared by everyone, would make the world a better place to
live.

Sadly, we live in an imperfect world and it is best to establish that
fact clearly in your mind, if improvement in your emotional intelligence
remains your goal.

People do not listen to angry people who shout and demand we
change our behavior. Instead, under those circumstances, people are more
likely to defend their behavior than to change it. If you can process your
shoulds, oughts, musts, have tos and *needs* in a way that makes your message
more appealing, people may be more likely to listen to you.

When you speak to me that way, I don't like it.

Do something about it.

I am.

****

This Is NOT Easy: This process of improving your emotional
intelligence is drawn out and often tiresome. At first you might actually
believe you are decreasing your emotional intelligence, rather than
improving it. That's because everything you will be doing (and thinking) is
new and has to be built from the ground up. When you do new things,
you are often not going to immediately master them. You will fail at your
first attempts to do some things, but, over time, you will begin to succeed
more often than you fail.

****

not a process for becoming emotionless. This

...otional intelligence is designed to address

...ebilitating or overwhelming, like rage,

...mally you can identify those emotions

...ou (and others) and how they interfere

...y living. This entire process of improving your

...al intelligence by improving your thinking will be devoted to

unmanageable beliefs and emotions that you will attempt to reconcile and

make less self-defeating. If you are feeling sadness, unhappiness or ennui,

it may be simply a healthy expression of disappointment. Learn the

lessons that disappointment can provide, rather than trying to escape

them. Of course, you might also use this time for learning to better

understand your emotions and how you create them through your

crooked and self-defeating thinking.

****

A Lifetime Goal: You are embarking on a journey for life. This

improvement you are about to make in your emotional intelligence isn't

something you can do for a while and then come back to later. Teaching

your brain how to work differently will take a lot of effort and a lot of

time. Don't beat yourself up when you fail. Use your new way of thinking

to help adjust to your failures and move forward.

> *I can forgive myself when I fail. I am a work in progress.*
>
> *I will not be perfect in my lifetime, so I am not even going to try anymore.*
>
> *I am a combination of strengths and weaknesses.*
>
> *I can live peacefully among others knowing they may not live up to my*
expectations of them.

It will take the force of will to do that.

STRATEGY THREE

Kleenex

Part of my clinical training required that I actually be a client seeking help from a therapist. That expectation of my program was built from the idea that a better-informed therapist would be one who knew what it was like to sit in the client's seat, to have an *in-vivo* (in life) educational experience. So I sought out a therapist to fulfill my 10-hour/10 session obligation. I began by registering with the student counseling center and getting a therapist assigned to me.

"Do you have a preference?"

"A preference?"

"Oh, most folks have a preference for a male or a female therapist. Do you have a preference?"

"Can you recommend one?"

"Not sure. I think they're all pretty much the same. Have a seat, please. We'll just go with the luck of the draw. Let me see who's available."

The counseling center was as one might expect - a former Victorian style, single family home with a zillion painted-over fireplaces, retro-fitted cubby-spaces that nicely transformed the building into awkwardly meandering faculty and therapy offices. Paint peeled from the ceilings and hung like stalactites. A faint, musty odor hung in the air. A bulky staircase covered in dusty, aged yellow shag carpet hulked behind the over-sized double front doors. Posters of kittens and rainbows were stapled to the waiting room walls, imprinted with slogans like, *Even if happiness forgets you a little bit, never completely forget about it* and *The best way to cheer yourself up is to try to cheer up somebody else.* Of course, there was the old standby (the emergency poster) detailing how some ethereal being carried some guy across the beach and turned two sets of footprints into one. The coffee table was strewn with old *Cosmopolitan* magazines: *Is your Boyfriend Right for You? Find out in 5 minutes!* A box of Kleenex was set precisely beside each chair.

The therapist began by asking me how she could help me. Her body language was somewhat animated, spirited, as if she were preparing to open a surprise Christmas present on her lap.

"I'm not really sure," I said, "I have this class assignment to speak with a counselor for ten hours, so here I am." I handed her my assignment sheet.

"Oh, yes! How nice," she said, handing my paper back to me with the enthusiasm one would show when giving a dog a new toy. I moved back in my chair. "We get these all the time. I'm a student too. I'm sure we can find something to discuss. Do you have anything in mind?"

I thought for a moment, literally placing my finger on my temple. "Well, I don't like it that I am losing my hair. Is that worth talking about?"

The therapist immediately reached for the box of Kleenex, "That's something," she said and cleared her throat, "How does that make you feel?"

"I feel like an old guy. Like, I'm only 23, but I feel like I look 53."

"You look wonderful." She leaned forward and grasped my hand, "You're a very handsome man . . . boy. Have you thought of wearing a cap?"

"Not really. I sweat a lot."

"How about a hairpiece? I hear *Hair Club for Men* performs miracles."

"I'm 23."

She leaned forward, as if preparing to tell me I had twelve minutes to live. She lowered her voice. "You have a *self-esteem* problem. The first thing we have to do is get you to a place where you don't care what people think of your hair."

"Where is that place?"

"Well, silly, we have to make a list of all your positive qualities and focus more on those things than on your weaker qualities. Do you have any positive qualities?"

"I already feel pretty good about my positive qualities."

She looked at me, troubled with my answer. "Sounds to me like you're in denial."

"Goodness, really?"

"Yes! It sounds like you might be *splitting* or maybe you have like a *personality disorder*. Sort of like a *dissociative identity*. It's called DID. It's nothing to worry about, really." She patted my knee. "I've seen this sort of thing before. I will have to consult with my clinical supervisor, but you might need more than 10 sessions."

****

17

I remember sitting in a booth at the student center cafeteria, eating my lunch, several weeks after my first session with the therapist. I was reading a book on DID, astonished at the uncanny similarities between myself and the diagnosis. (Later in my education, I noticed that nearly any diagnosis I read about matched my personality – schizophrenia, borderline personality, oppositional defiance, bi-polar. You name it; I had it. I listened to the two women sitting in the booth behind me, talking about their feelings and what one of them was doing to get over her depression.

"So what's up now? I thought you were getting better."

"No, I'm still depressed."

"Again?"

"Yeah."

"What happened to your therapist?"

"He broke up with me."

"That's OK," she said, "You're cute. You'll find a new one."

STRATEGY FOUR

I know what you're thinking

Ah-ha! moments are crucial to expanding our knowledge of something. Ah-ha! s often come when they're least expected. For example, I was preparing to slice a lemon and, in the middle of making the first incision, my mind awakened to a new understanding of emotional wellness. *Ah-ha!* I realized that just looking at the lemon caused me to experience the taste of it.

My lips pursed.

My tongue and cheeks salivated.

My teeth clenched.

While slicing it into wedges, I wondered if I could cause myself to taste something else – to fight against the thought of the lemon and conjure, say the taste of watermelon or a ham sandwich. Could I *control* my imagination in such a way that it *prevented* my *involuntarily response* to the lemon? Or was it just, automatic – out of my control?

***

Ah-ha! moments as you may well know are unexpected bolts of insight, surprises. Like when you realize something for the first time. Ah-ha! moments can be those episodes in your life you might call *lasting impressions*. Ah-ha! moments are rarely, if ever, forgotten. My first Ah-ha! came when I was around five. I realized that counting to 100 wasn't hard, once I learned to count to ten. As I grew older, Ah-ha! moments came one right after another. Five, six, ten . . . tad poles came from that jelly stuff in the swamp. You can catch bumble bees and not get stung if you have a mayonnaise jar and a lid. You cannot break a Coke bottle with your bare foot without paying a high price. If you stepped on a nail the blood would soak an entire beach towel on the way to the hospital.

Ah-ha!

At fifteen, I was capable of multiple Ah-ha! moments in a day.

I had a significant Ah-ha! moment when I decided to study health psychology – when I learned to think about psychological conditions biologically. This level of Ah-ha! is often referred to as the life changing Ah-ha! Like the Ah-ha! you have when you find the one you will love forever, or when you finally decide on a career or a course in life.

The discovery of *health psychology* was my professional Ah-ha moment! Health psychology is a system for bringing together biology, behavior and social context to better understand health and emotional illness. My first health psychology professor was a very stoic, curmudgeon type. He made it clear that providing mental health assistance was not possible without making a *complete assessment* of an individual's biological, sociological and psychological state.

From my professor's perspective, people are best viewed in terms of their sum total, rather than their component parts. In actual fact, every part of the human organism interacts with every other part of itself. The mind and the body are interconnected and should never be viewed as separate.

My professor took off his tweed jacket and hung it on the back of his chair. He looked out over the classroom and went on to tell an amazing story about a man who literally lived on a golf course in Pennsylvania. The man was unexpectedly stricken with some rather extraordinary behavior, after finishing up the 15th hole. (On the 16th hole, he apparently removed his clothes, climbed onto the lower limb of a horse chestnut tree and chattered like a squirrel). There was no history of mental health problems in his family. Yet, according the EMT's report, he was displaying all of the classic signs of *schizophrenia*.

Long story short, after interviewing his golf pals, it was discovered that the man had a habit of putting his golf tee back into his mouth, if it weren't broken, after teeing off. As unappealing as it may seem, the dirty tee was picking up the pesticides in the ground. After 15 holes, the amount of pesticide in his system reached a level that implicated his nervous system.

Voila! the likeness of schizophrenia.

If his doctors had viewed him entirely from a mental health perspective, we may never have heard from the man again. He may have been institutionalized, placed on psychotropic medications, labeled a nut and stored like so much grain in a silo! I could see the energy bubbling inside my professor, "Instead, he was treated holistically. He was evaluated from head to toe, mind, body and soul! An analysis was made of his vital functions, as well as his emotional status. More importantly, he was subjected to a blood screening, which discovered the pollutant in his system. He didn't have a mental health condition after all. He was a victim of poisoning!" His lecture was reminiscent of Sherlock Holmes identifying the killer from a lineup of suspects.

***

People tend to separate mind from body and set about treating them as if they had no connection to one another. There was pure joy on my professor's face. The twinkle in his eyes, and his red, glee-filled, varicose cheeks was invigorating and instigated the growth of my Ah-ha! moment to the status of an awakening.

Now, as a lecturer myself, discussing these same, very-complex topics (often within the confines of an hour) leaves some of my audience in the dark. Being my own biggest fan, and wanting everyone to get as much enjoyment from my message as I do delivering it, I often use catchy slogans, attention-grabbers and other devices to help my message stick in the mind of my listeners. (Slogans, attention-grabbers and other devices are often the very things that bring about Ah-ha! moments.)

***

In my experience, Ah-ha! moments are more common among those who possess a vivid imagination. I am a big believer in the power of imagination. In fact, I have found that imagination, when used judiciously, allows for a better understanding of the world. Imagination can also lead to difficulties. For example, when we use imagination to interpret how others perceive us and how we interpret the motives of the people around us: *I know what you're thinking. I knew he was going to say that.*

Our understanding of the world, which is, in part, our imagination, guides us in how we choose to interact with groups, individuals and even ourselves. Our imagination can even impact our decision-making in both helpful and harmful ways. Because perception and imagination are decidedly similar, perception, like imagination, varies from person to person. It is, therefore, possible for people to feel utterly different about the exact same situation, circumstance or event. Our reality is created in our imagination.

In my early days as a therapist, a client once asked me if he could talk about his mother's recent death, "Sure," I said, "I am sorry to hear she died. That must be tough for you."

"On second thought, can we change the subject? Talk about something else?"

"Sure, may I ask why? We just got started."

"Because I don't feel the way you are describing it. It hasn't been tough for me at all. In fact, I'm angry. And I'm embarrassed every time someone assumes I am unhappy about her death."

Even meaning that we think is broadly held can vary from person to person.

**

People have the potential to apply any number of different meanings to their encounters with others. The ingestion of poison, the death of a parent, the loss of property, even the weather can carry more than one connotation; evoke more than one emotional reaction:

Ugh, it's raining.

I wish it would rain every day. I love rain.

I hate it. It is just so depressing.

It brings me to life.

**

The conscious awareness of how one goes about expressing an emotional reaction is the substance of centuries of literature and philosophy. Beginning with the premise that, because we bring our own meaning to everything we experience, there are few *natural* reactions to any event; few *natural* emotions. Emotion, oddly, is *mostly* learned responses; emotional choices.

Epictetus tells us that *men are disturbed not by things, but by the view which they take of them.* Making the connection between our physical bodies, our social experiences our thoughts, beliefs, feelings and behaviors are all essential to improving emotional intelligence. More essential, however, will be the identification of where emotions live, how they are formed, how they are maintained and how they are defended. Epictetus also tells us that no *great thing is created suddenly*, so be patient. For me, all this philosophy and more came from a single Ah-ha! moment – one involving a lemon and a jelly bean. This particular Ah-ha! moment changed my whole understanding of emotion and how I can help others improve their emotional intelligence. This Ah-ha! moment is the impetus for writing this book.

We shall return to this mind-altering event in a bit.

STRATEGY FIVE

What are your beliefs?

The word *belief* is often synonymous with the word *religion –
religious belief.* Although religion is responsible for a great number of our
individual and cultural beliefs, it is not the primary source of the beliefs
we will be discussing in this book. I make this point early because I am
accustomed to hearing people declare that they have no intention of
giving up their religion for the sake of improving their emotional
intelligence. Our discussion of beliefs will have little to do with religion,
so relax. We will not be discussing things you believe *in*, but instead your
beliefs *about* yourself, others and the world around you. Those topics are
often related, but it will be up to you to make that connection and that
distinction.

What are your beliefs?

Your beliefs are your *confident ideas*, your premises for truth, your
values, morals and the legitimacy you place in law. If something is within

your awareness, you will already have a belief about it, or you will advance a belief to attach to it.

He stood me up again.

Again?

Yup, what should I do with him? He makes me so mad! I should kill him.

He has no right to keep doing that to you. I think you should break up with him.

Break up with him! No way, he does a lot of nice things for me.

You shouldn't allow anyone to treat you that way, no matter what they do to make up for it.

You're right.

Ah-ha! The birth of a new belief.

You use your beliefs to determine *goodness* and *badness*, from a boyfriend's behavior to how you appreciate art and music. You have beliefs in your expectations of others, what they *should* think, how they *must* live, what they *have to* eat and who they *need* to love, all a result of exposure within a culture.

All of your rules, your *should, oughts, musts, have tos* and *needs* are learned. They are not facts or imperatives. They are opinions confused as facts.

You accumulated your beliefs by internalizing the values, morals and the meanings of the things that have happened in your life and the *expectations* you have of the people around you. Over time, you become very clear about these sorts of things.

Your belief system represents a form of knowledge, one that allows you and others to comfortably live and work within a social structure. The expression of your beliefs is a demonstration to others that you are accepting an agreed-upon system. Some of the more established, familiar beliefs you might hold or will encounter might include:

- *The belief that your emotions come from how others interact with you* and *that your happiness* and *unhappiness come from external sources – from other people and things.*

- *The belief that you must be appreciated* and *shown respect by others in order to live happily.*

- *The belief that life is horrible or awful because things are not the way you want them to be.*

- *The belief that you and others should be thoroughly competent* and *intelligent at all times.*

- *The belief that because something once strongly affected your life, it will affect it forever.*

- *The belief that you must have control over everything that affects you.*

- *The belief that you have virtually no control over your emotions* and *that you cannot help feeling disturbed.*

If you can fashion your emotional language, your self-talk to combat these beliefs, you will be well on your way to improved emotional intelligence. In time, using your new beliefs to navigate your world, you will develop *sustainable* methods to maintain them and how to enforce them when interacting with others. Disappointment and frustration often result when your expectations are not being met for how you believe others should, ought, must, have to and need to behave. You will notice that your *upsettedness* is often related to how others ignore the morals, values and expectations you hold. People are likely to follow their own rules and often ignore yours. Although these traditionally held, generally accepted beliefs are often articulated clearly within a culture, they are also often identifiable in self-talk, or the emotional language you use to legitimize how you suppose things *should, ought, must, has to* and *need* to be. Your self-talk is your inner attempt to interpret what you perceive. Your self-talk attempts to fit the observable behavior into your established understanding of the world. Emotional problems are likely to arise when you place greater emphasis on *your own* belief than on *fact*. The fact often is, however, that your beliefs, although useful for you, are not always useful at the moment to others. Emotional intelligence depends on your ability to reconcile these two notions.

What are the *facts in your self-talk*; what are your *beliefs*?

***

I once worked with a man using the techniques and philosophies we are discussing. The man, like many of us, had problems with anyone who stood behind a counter. A sales clerks, fast food cashiers, complaint desk attendants, social service providers, gas station attendants, anyone who is in a position to help customers. His traditional mindset was to approach cautiously. "You never know what you're gonna get. I stay clear of 'em."

"What do you mean?"

"Well they don't greet you. They stare at you and just look through you, waiting for you to say something. I just hate it. I know they will do that, so I just go into it with that in my head. Last week it took me nine telephone calls to the same telephone operator to get her to fax me something."

"What do you tell yourself when you enter a shop that has a cashier?"

"I am pissed before I even get into the store."

"What do you tell yourself?"

"I tell myself that people who work behind counters should not be stupid and rude and will always give me a hard time. They should care more and they need to get some manners. I can't stand it when they act that way and I need respect in order to have a two-way conversation with someone."

"How do you suppose those thoughts help you get through transactions with counter people?"

"I am angry before I even go in there."

"What can you tell yourself instead?"

"I can tell myself that each experience is new and different."

"Anything else?"

"I can tell myself that I can stand it when people don't act the way I think they should act. I can be less angry and more patient. I can tell myself that I want people to behave differently and not that I need it."

Our goal when improving our emotional intelligence is to locate our thoughts, our beliefs, and challenge them, using a process of *balanced evaluation*. We can evaluate how our self talk is helping us manage the emotional task we want to achieve. Our self talk must accommodate the emotional result we are seeking. If we want to be angry when we experience adversity, we will. If we want to be less angry, we will. If we want to feel unhappy, sad, forgiving or pardoning, we will. We first have to change the way we think about adversity.

It will take the force of will to do that.

STRATEGY SIX

The force of will

Our early training, especially our training in language, the very thing that connects each of us to one another, does not (without immense difficulty) accommodate the phrases, *I make myself feel. I made myself angry. I really pissed myself off today.*

We learn early in our lives that when we express displeasure, we do so in a way that projects the source of our emotion onto something external of ourselves, traditionally onto others. Our language, both internal and external, is developed more in line with:

You made me feel unhappy.

He made me mad.

She makes me sick.

They make everyone feel uneasy.

These are very common, well understood, easily accommodated phrases.

Few would stop and question the logic of these statements.

We are trained and encouraged, through language, thought and behavior to attribute our emotions to something external of ourselves.

Likewise, we often don't even attribute our own joys and successes to ourselves, without promoting the idea that our happiness wouldn't be possible without the help of others:

I am successful; you made me successful.

I won this award; God gave me this award.

I am angry; you made me angry.

I am depressed; he made me depressed.

I am sick to my stomach; she made me sick.

While we look outside ourselves, at the people and things around us as the source of our negative, self-defeating emotions, we wait for them to change their behavior, so we can be happy.

How can I help you today?

My husband is mean to me.

How can I help you with that?

You can make him come home and stop staying out all night.

I can't do that. Maybe you can ask him to come in and talk.

He doesn't want to change.

How can I help you?

The problem is that while we are searching for answers to why we feel the way we do, we are less likely to search in the very place our emotions live.

Within our own heads!

As we grow and age, we develop our emotional competence. Unfortunately, our assessment of our emotional competence is judged against how successful we have been at taking responsibility for the feelings of everyone around us. Most people remain in the same emotional furrow their entire lives, living and reliving their emotions in exactly the same way, every time something happens, feeling confident that their emotional response is the only one available under the circumstances. Improvement in emotional intelligence requires the consideration of other emotional options, leading to more life-sustaining, self-enhancing emotional decisions.

Our emotions embody and express the ideas, truths and stories we learn from others. If we believe that the only recourse for people who treat us badly is to shout, criticize, hit and belittle, it is time to learn that there really are other options.

***

I often tell my students that the toughest feature of trying to live sanely and rationally is that most people believe that they and others *make everyone feel* emotion. As if we lived in a culture of magicians and sorcerers. The fact is, people perceive what others do and say, and they make judgments about those behaviors. They think about them, and they generate an emotion that they believe is supportive of their judgment.

> *She said I was fat.*
> *How dare she say that to you? After all you did for her?*
> *She is a stupid head.*
> *You should tell her off.*

If we choose to *forgive* or pardon people for their poor choices, rather than ranting and raving about the injustice of it all, we will not express unmanaged anger and be more likely to express managed displeasure, discomfort and unhappiness. In that frame of mind, we are more likely to express our disapproval and be heard.

> *She said I was fat.*
> *How dare she say that to you? After all you did for her?*
> *She sometimes says things that are insensitive. Maybe I am a bit plump, anyway. I do like her. She wasn't lying. She has so few friends. I feel sorry for her. I think I will tell her how I feel.*
> *What are you talking about!? I'd pull a knife on her!*

Generation after generation we teach our children that their emotions come from the way other people treat them. They learn from the start to attribute their feelings to things outside of themselves. Under these circumstances, launching a new mindset, after years of training, is made so much more difficult. Changing the shape of the human mind is less painful when it is fresh and more impressionable. If you have children, you might begin to use the lessons in this book to start your child's emotional training. You might begin by helping them learn to take ownership of their emotions.

I remember working with a woman, employing the skills we are discussing. She had a very young son, and started teaching him her new-found philosophy very early. *Mommy didn't make you unhappy. You made yourself unhappy. You can't always get your own way. You can be patient instead. You can make a better choice. What better choice could you have made?*

You may be thinking, *How can a child understand these concepts?* Well, it's easy.

Children have to *hear* the concepts and they will begin to *assimilate* the concepts into the way they think and feel. Just like they hear the nutty ideas we teach them now. Over time, this philosophy becomes the framework from which children understand their world.

Once my friend's child started first grade, all was well; until his teacher said, "You shouldn't do that! You are a bad boy! Bad!" to which the child replied, "I am not a bad boy. I made a poor choice. I will try to make a better choice next time."

This child has never ceased to amaze me. He is now a well-rounded, confident and emotionally stable young man.

You have to begin somewhere.

It's best to begin here and now and as early as possible.

We are wired to adapt to emotional challenges, at any age. Nature makes it inevitable that we cooperate, if not simply for survival. Your goal to improve your emotional intelligence, however, is not to adapt to society's prevailing opinion.

It is to act against it.

Your challenge then will be to improve your emotional intelligence while living in a world where most people reject the idea that they create their own feelings. As you try to change and maintain your new internal logic, you will still have to go to work, shop, interact with people at the movie theatre and drive a car, making the process bewildering and often lonely.

I am reminded of a time when I was leaving a meeting and a woman stopped me to tell me how I *made* her so angry.

"Goodness, how?" I asked.

"You disagreed with me," she said, "On that issue about healthcare."

"That made you angry?"

"Of course it did. I think my position was very clear. How would you feel?"

As I listened to her, I imagined myself *unmaking* her anger. I imagined waving a magic wand over her head and making her happy. For, wouldn't it be logical to think that if I could *make* her angry, I could also *make* her happy?

"I guess I could have agreed with you, instead," I said.

"Yes, that would have been a whole lot better. You also embarrassed me."

"The extent of my power over you is unsettling."

"What?"

"I'm sorry."

We must interact with misinformed people, people who think we make them feel, and we must talk like them, if we want to get along. But, once you begin to make improvement in your emotional intelligence, NEVER again think like them!

***

Sadly, the more you increase your emotional intelligence, and the saner you become, you still have to live in close quarters with the misinformed. They own most everything, they are often the objects of our affection and they are decidedly in control of much of the world's food supply. So you should learn to appease them, at every turn, in order to survive. Repeat after me: *I'm sorry to make you unhappy. I'm sorry to make you angry. I'm sorry to make you feel anything but happiness. Your emotions are my burden in life. Your emotions are my responsibility. I promise to handle your emotions more delicately in the future and provide you with ample opportunity for happiness, even if it means I will have to be unhappy forever.*

***

It's hard to say how many magical, externally focused concepts have been allowed to flourish within our culture, our language and ostensibly, our species. It could be that our ancestors needed a certain level of illogical thinking and behaving in order to achieve cooperation within a tribe.

"Mongo made me so mad. He stole my totem again."

"Mongo! You have to stop stealing! You make people mad!"

"Yeah, if he doesn't stop we will make him feel sorry!"

"You hear that, Mongo? You're a very bad boy! You make people feel angry. Stop it!"

We speak to one another, live with one another and cooperate with one another in a way that accommodates insanity.

Who really knows why?

Suffice it to know that it is not a life-enhancing behavior.

∗∗∗

Yesterday, while in the men's room, I noticed a lot of dried mud on the floor. It appeared that whoever had previously used the commode had obviously ridden motocross and then cleaned his shoes where I was sitting. I contemplated the dirt, myself. The redness of the dirt and its clay-like quality interested me. (One of the pieces of dried clay looked a lot like Abraham Lincoln.) On my way back to my office, I saw one of the janitors lingering in a corner by the stairwell. I told her of the dirt on the floor. After returning to my office, I soon forgot about it, losing myself in my work. That afternoon, one of the secretaries in my department came to my cube.

"Can I talk to you about something?"

"Yes, come in. Please," I said, motioning her to sit.

The woman stood before me, hands clasped. She said, "Would you please apologize to Betty?"

"Who's Betty?"

"She's one of the ladies who cleans up. The janitor-lady."

"Why on earth would I apologize to Betty?"

"For the mess you made in the bathroom."

I stared for a moment, "I didn't make the mess. I reported it."

"She's all torn up about the mess. She had to sweep it up and mop the floor. She had to take an emergency smoke break. She's as mad as a bee. You really *made* her mad."

"Did I?"

"Why won't you just apologize? She will feel a lot better if you did."

It will take the force of will to change this nut-headedness.

STRATEGY SEVEN

The ABCs of Emotion

I use the ABCs to keep track of my emotions. Not just my own, but everyone's emotions, generally. The ABCs rely on the theory that human beings derive emotion from thought. If we can find a way to chart our emotional development, to create a visual representation of how we came to think and feel what we are emoting, we can get a clearer more manageable picture of what we've done to create our own emotions and what we can do to change them.

Learning the ABCs is much like, well, learning the ABCs.

Using them is the tough part.

Get a piece of paper and write on it:

A: *Activating* Event

B: *Belief*

C: Emotional *Consequence*

D: *Disputation*

E: Emotional *Evolution*

This will be the format from which you will derive your current and future improved emotional intelligence.

Who knew?

The A in the ABCs identifies the *activating event*. The activating event designates that *something happened* and it caught your attention. It is a description of the event you want to better manage. Some examples may be:

- *Your boss criticized you.*
- *Someone was disrespectful toward you.*
- *Your neighbor cuts down your new bushes with a Weed Eater.*
- *Your husband says he doesn't love you anymore.*
- *Your service at a restaurant wasn't quite what you expected.*

Write down your activating event in the space provided for the Activating Event (A).

***

The B is the belief you apply to the activating event (A):

- *People should never criticize me. If they do, I am a bad person and I can't stand that.*
- *People should show me respect when they talk to me. If they don't, they should be damned.*
- *People should never make errors in judgment. If they do, they are assholes.*
- *If my husband doesn't love me, I am entirely unlovable.*
- *Wait people should always treat me as a valued customer. If they don't, I cannot enjoy my food.*

These are all fairly common beliefs (B) that often lead to quite unfortunate emotional consequences.

Let's explore the activating event (A): *My boss criticized me.* Your belief (B) may be that your boss was harsh with you and he *shouldn't* be harsh with you. You may believe you *need* your boss' appreciation in order to feel good about yourself and your employment. You might even believe that you *must* be treated nicely by your boss and your coworkers, in order to achieve happiness in your job and in your life. The B (the belief) is the *self-talk* you use to tell yourself what to think about the event (A).

The B is best understood in terms of how you use the words *should, ought, must, have to* and *need* to apply *meaning* to the A.

(A) The cashier is rude to me.

(B) Cashiers should always be friendly. I cannot stand it when they aren't.

(A) My husband criticized me.

(B) Husbands should never criticize their wives. I need my husband to show me respect all the time. My husband must never behave badly with me.

(A) I failed my test.

(B) I shouldn't fail tests. If I do, I am stupid. I need to pass all tests in order to be viewed as intelligent. I must be above-average intelligence in order to be intelligent at all.

***

The C in this paradigm represents the *emotional consequence* you have, after something happens (A) and you think about it (B).

In simple terms, something happens (A) and you have a fleeting thought / belief (B). That THOUGHT must be captured, because that thought is the VERY THING that caused your emotional reaction (C) to the thing that happened (A). If you would rather not be angry, depressed, fearful, and anxious or worried, you can do something about it. You can change the thought/belief (B).

(A) The cashier is rude to me.

(B) Cashiers *should* always be friendly. I *cannot stand it* when they are rude and insensitive.

(C) I am *angry*.

(A) My husband criticized me.

(B) Husbands *should never* criticize their wives.

(C) I am *angry* and *afraid*.

(A) I failed my test.

(B) I *shouldn't* fail tests. If I do, *I am stupid*.

(C) I am *afraid* and *depressed*.

***

Remember, you will not have an emotion (C) unless you have a belief (B) about the activating event (A). For example, if you believe you *should*, at all times, be treated well by your boss, you are likely to be angry when s/he doesn't treat you the way you tell yourself you NEED to be treated. People do not become upset simply because something happens. They become upset because they tell themselves something about what happened: A + B = C.

The beliefs that we hold are both *explicit* and *implicit* philosophical assumptions about events, personal desires and preferences. If our beliefs are rigid and absolutistic, they are considered *dysfunctional*, leading only to a place of enduring unhappiness. If you believe that your happiness (B) depends on others behaving the way you demand that they behave (B), you will likely experience one misfortune after another (C) when people behave contrary to your beliefs (A).

***

We've talked about the similarity between learning a foreign language and learning a new *emotional language*. When we speak to ourselves in terms of what *should, ought, must* and *has to be* in order for us to be happy in our lives, we are imposing the inevitability of unmanageable, self-defeating and destructive emotional consequences on ourselves – when things don't work out the way we demand they should. Your goal is to change your personal beliefs, demands and needs to manageable *wants* and *flexible* and *constructive preferences*.

I remember a student who sat in on one of my lectures. "I don't get it," she said.

"Well, if you tell yourself you NEED what you WANT you will be quite unhappy, maybe even angry, if you don't get it."

"I tell myself I NEED what I really WANT – A LOT."

"Possibly."

"If I tell myself I NEED people to respect me, I will be pretty pissed when I don't get respect. If I tell myself I WANT people to respect me, it isn't the end of the world if they don't give me what I want. I might just be sad when they don't respect me. If I think I NEED it, I might even kill to get it. It might take a while, but I can learn to think about it this way."

***

The ABC framework assumes that humans have both innate rational and irrational potentials. We possess an innate drive to express *attachment* and *fear*, if not for any other reason than to survive as a species. We build on *attachment* and *fear* through our exposure within a specific culture. For example, *respect* (a learned emotion) cannot be succinctly

41

defined because it is derived from *attachment* (our basic emotion) and varies between cultures.

> *You are not showing me much respect.*
>
> *Of course I am.*
>
> *Not the kind of respect I am familiar with.*
>
> *What can I do to help you feel respected?*

Knowing the basic ABCs is where improving your emotional intelligence begins. Identifying self-defeating thoughts (self-talk) that are *rigid, extreme, unrealistic, illogical* and *absolutist* is your goal. Once you are able to identify your self-talk (beliefs), you will then begin to forcefully and actively question and dispute them, replacing them with a new emotional language; a language that is more adaptive to more stable mental health.

You have a choice to make yourself feel healthily by thinking healthily.

***

It took a while for me to apply the ABCs to my own life, to the point where it made only a modicum of difference. Remember, I knew what the ABCs were meant to represent. I just met an array of unexpected challenges when I tried to use them. The following Five Lessons are imparted from my early experience and may help reduce the amount of time you spend learning, using and understanding the ABCs:

- LESSON ONE: Not every human emotion is self-defeating and worth examining with the ABCs. Just because it's uncomfortable does not mean it has to be run through the ABCs. Instead, you might just want to try to increase your *frustration tolerance*. Endure. Be a candidate for the change you hope for in others.

  An emotion must be *unmanageable* to process it through the ABCs. Anger can take on unmanageable proportions, but not all anger is a candidate for the ABCs. Some anger is very manageable, somewhat motivating and often quickly dissipates. Some forms of love are unmanageable. If you are expressing obsessive love, it may be time to work through that issue. It can easily become unmanageable anger. Regardless, it is important to know that when we use the ABCs, we focus on the *unmanageability* of emotion, not the elimination of emotion from our lives.

- LESSON TWO: It is not your goal to become *emotionless*. Emotion is an essential part of your human existence. It might be your goal, instead, to celebrate your unique character and the array of emotional experiences you can have with others. We can and should celebrate all that we are, emotionally, if we are to achieve a fulfilling and complete life. *Ridding ourselves of emotion is not our goal.* Nor is it possible, without surgery. And even then it is a precarious operation. Managing unmanageable emotions is your goal. Celebrate your emotional beauty! *Try not to make your emotional sameness with others the standard by which you judge yourself.* Enjoy yourself and learn to *forgive yourself.*

- LESSON THREE: It takes dedication to get the most out of the ABC system. The paradigm will make sense at face value – if you look it over, it doesn't take a long time to conceptualize it. The practice of the ABCs, however, is the tough part. Think about the years upon years you've spent developing your *roles* and *scripts.* You learn to play roles and their related scripts for nearly any emotional situation you encounter. You have to rid yourself of those roles and scripts that are harmful, unhealthy and self-defeating. You can replace them with more manageable, rational and flexible thoughts and behaviors.

- LESSON FOUR: It's as if there are containers of dusty roles and scripts floating round in your head. You can imagine throwing a match on them and watching them go up in flames. That can be your sign that you have to start to build new ones. If you don't practice, if you fall back into your old emotional language, you won't achieve your desired results. Changing the way you think and behave will be the most important thing you can do to build your emotional strength. The more you practice, the more energy you dedicate to delivering healthier emotional information to your brain, the closer you will get to your preferred result.

- LESSON FIVE: It takes patience to achieve your new emotional milestones. Don't beat yourself up when you fail at achieving your improved emotional intelligence. Your skills with the ABCs cannot be developed quickly or immediately. You have to commit to achieving results over the long haul. Quick fixes never work, so don't expect any. It takes a plan, dedication, and proper attitude to get the results that you are looking for. Without the personal commitment to the task, you'll give up before you reach your goal. Be diligent, focused and patient. With the proper dedication and the right attitude, which is the best way to build your emotional intelligence, you will make steady recognizable progress to reaching your mental health goals.

It will take the force of will to do this.

STRATEGY EIGHT

The D and *the* E

After learning the ABCs, you may want to run out and tell everyone about them.

Don't be too hasty.

There is still the D and E to learn.

Before we discuss the D and the E of the ABCs, I want to acknowledge from the beginning that a great deal more work will go into discovering the D.

The D requires skill, dexterity and dedication to master.

Albert Ellis, the grandfather of cognitive behavior therapy and the father of rational emotive behavior therapy, introduced me to this ABC logic. At the time, the ABC message was the single most important bit of information I had ever learned. When it came to learning the rest of the system, the D in particular, I met my enduring challenge.

I started much the same way you have. I purchased many books, and I read them diligently, thoroughly, *voraciously*. But the more I read the more complicated things seemed to become. Talking about the D with friends and classmates was troubling, to say the least.

"I didn't make you mad," I learned to say. "You made yourself mad."

"You just took one of my nuggets."

"Yes, but it wasn't that I took your nugget that *made* you mad. It was what you told yourself about me taking your nugget. What did you tell yourself when I helped myself to your food?"

"I was telling myself that I am really hungry and I want to eat my own food."

"What else were you telling yourself?"

"I was telling myself you are being an asshole and I am going to beat you with my shoe if you don't get it together."

The ABCs made thinking about my emotional issues less problematic, far more functional and more *action oriented*. But the D continued to present me with difficulties. Regardless, just the first three letters of the ABC paradigm gave me a level of emotional confidence I never had before. I felt in charge of ME! I found I could only apply my newfound skills in a world that didn't understand what I was trying to achieve. The ABCs provided me with a clear path toward sanity. It seemed to drive everyone else away, "You are really making me mad."

"I am not making you mad. You are making yourself mad."

"Shut the *$%$* up."

"OK."

***

So what is this D?

- The D represents the necessary process of *disputing* your beliefs. Discovering your *should, oughts, musts, have tos* and *needs* and locating the logic you use to hold on to them.

- The D is a time for testing what you tell yourself; for locating the rationale of continuing to think the way you do about yourself and others.

- The D is an active process of asking yourself the right questions to get at the right answers to evolve your emotion to something more manageable.

- The D, when used correctly, will help you confront your irrational beliefs, vigorously compelling you to recognize the irrationalities in your thinking and your self-defeating emotional consequences (C) to activating events (A).

At D you will ask yourself if your belief is actually true, or is it some ideal you would like others to live by? Is your belief really a rule that everyone has to live by, or is it a behavior you demand from others?

- *Do I really need cooperation from others to be happy in my life?*
- *Can I live with it when people act against my wishes?*
- *Is it really so unbearable when I don't get what I expect?*
- *Is this something I WANT or something I think I NEED?*
- *Where is the evidence for this belief?*
- *Can I prove that this belief is true?*

Disputing (D) your thoughts and beliefs (B) is a learned technique that, like using the ABCs, is an acquired skill that takes practice. Disputation (D) provides an opportunity to make new judgments about familiar dilemmas. By challenging your customary self-talk, your roles and scripts (B), you can actually see how you create your own emotions (C) and, by disputing (D) the thoughts that lead to the emotional consequence (C), impede the generation of unhealthy, unproductive emotion.

- *If I tell myself that not getting what I want is horrible, awful and that I cannot stand it, I will feel that way.*

- *If I tell myself I can stand it when I don't get what I want and that I can actually be happy under those circumstances I will feel sad and, at the most, uncomfortable.*

***

Disputing (D) requires you to *challenge your firmly-held beliefs.* We might ask ourselves to provide *evidence*, a *factual basis* for our beliefs.

- Ask yourself to *prove*, for example, that people should be respectful of you.
- *Prove* that your wife shouldn't divorce you.
- *Prove* that your children should not forget your birthday.

The only possible evidence for your belief is that *you don't like it* or *you would rather have it your way.* That is hardly enough evidence to expect others to change their behavior.

***

IMPORTANT NOTICE: Building your skill with disputing (D) will require that you remember what the word *should* implies and acknowledge the dangers implicit in using this word.

The word *should* gives support to your notion that YOU are the guardian of truth, right and wrong, good and bad.

Should is YOUR standard of excellence.

Should is YOUR standard of perfect.

Should is YOUR standard of ideal behavior that you impose on yourself and others.

- *You shouldn't talk that way to your father.*
- *You should be more loving.*
- *I should have done better on that test.*
- *I should be more flexible with the rules I apply to others.*

***

When you impose the words *should, ought, must, have to* and *need* on anything and anyone (including yourself), you are imposing a faultless standard on people and things. Instead, it may be best to impose your standard of best behavior on *yourself*. In that way, you can have some level of control in your own life and leave others to their own choices.

Using this philosophy can have its flaws.

Even you don't meet the standard of perfection you set for everyone around you. You may just have to learn to forgive yourself and others more often.

***

Shoulds, oughts, musts, have tos and *needs* are the inflexible demands you place on yourself and others. If you want to put some flexibility in these words, you can substitute them with the word *want*. Replacing your absolute, inflexible demands with *desires* and *want*s will likely provide you with far more evidence to support your self-talk.

***

In truth, each of your should, oughts, musts, have tos and needs are dysfunctional by-products of your upbringing. They are a reflection of how your culture expected you to behave ideally within that particular culture. (If you've noticed, there are many should, oughts, musts, have tos and needs that are particular to the home you grew up in, the community you assimilated and the state you were raised to live in. It would be nice if people naturally behaved ideally, perfectly and that we all shared exactly the same ideals and beliefs.

We don't.

You might ask yourself, before judging any behavior as imperfect and hopelessly flawed, if it is fair to hold yourself or others to an ideal standard, when you know very well that humans have little or no potential to reach perfection.

(A) The cashier is rude to me.

(B) Cashiers *should* always be friendly. I *cannot stand it* when they are rude and insensitive.

(C) I am *angry*.

(D) Is it true that people must always be friendly to me? Is it true that I have to always be treated well to find happiness in my own life? Is it true that when people behave against my belief that they are entirely bad and must be damned? Where is the proof for all this stuff I am telling myself?

(A) My husband criticized me.

(B) Husbands *should never* criticize their wives.

(C) I am *angry* and *afraid*.

(D) Where is the evidence that my husband must always behave the way I demand? Is it true that even when I behave badly that my husband must always treat me nicely? Where is the evidence that my husband must always be perfect in order to be married to me?

(A) I failed my test.

(B) I *shouldn't* fail tests. If I do, *I am stupid*.

(C) I am *afraid*.

(D) How have I determined that failing is a clear sign that I entirely a failure? Is it true that if I am not good at everything I do that I am not good? Is it true that when I fail I should be damned? Is it true that I should always succeed at everything I do?

Your thoughts are the source of your emotions.

Beliefs that are self-defeating tend NOT to stand up to scrutiny.

Self-defeating thoughts ignore the positive, exaggerate the negative, distort reality and over-generalize. In order to begin to learn the skill of disputing, I will share with you some of the lessons I learned over the course of my life with the ABCs:

- LESSON ONE: When you find yourself in a troubling emotional circumstance, ask yourself to state in one sentence what happened: *My boss criticized me (A).*

- LESSON TWO: After encapsulating the event, ask yourself what emotion you're using to respond to the event: *Anger (C).*

- LESSON THREE: After recognizing your emotional reaction to the event, ask yourself what you believe about the event (B): *It means people should never criticize me. If they do, it is awful and horrible and I can't stand it. I need my boss' approval to be happy in my life and he must always give it to me.*

- LESSON FOUR: After discovering your initial self talk, ask yourself for additional meaning (B): *I failed and that means I am a failure. If I am a failure, I am worthless. If I am worthless I cannot be loved. If I cannot be loved, I will be lonely. If I am lonely I will be depressed. If I am depressed I will have no life worth living.*

- LESSON FIVE: After discovering what the event means to you, ask yourself if all that you believe can stand up to critical examination and more stable evaluation (D): *Is it true that if I fail, I am a failure destined to live a worthless and unremarkable life?*

- LESSON SIX: After discovering the weaknesses in your self-talk, ask yourself for the truth about what you are telling yourself (E):

The truth is I failed BUT I can still be happy in my life, even if my boss criticizes me. I can try harder next time, and maybe I will succeed. But even if I don't, that doesn't mean I am a worthless failure. I am a work in progress, and I am bound to fail from time to time. It might be better to get myself used to that.

- LESSON SEVEN: Pay close attention to how you apply the words *should, ought, must, have to* and *need* in your daily life. These words are demanding of a *perfect* and *ideal standard*. You might not be best served by expecting the perfect and ideal behavior from anyone – including yourself. If you get it, be thankful for it. If you don't, you can always remind yourself that you and others are likely to miss the perfect and ideal standard.

  It will take the strength of will to do this.

STRATEGY NINE

Evolving your emotion

The result of disputing self-defeating beliefs and replacing them with rational ones may bring about an emotional evolution (E). An emotional evolution (E) is simply the process of exchanging your emotional response to something more manageable.

Evolving your emotion.

The (E) will represent your improved, more manageable emotional response!

Improving your emotional intelligence depends on your ability to turn anger into sadness, frustration, tolerance, hopefulness or forgiveness. You can evolve to any number of emotional reactions that are more suitable for happiness simply by disputing and evolving your thinking.

(A) The cashier is rude to me.

(B) Cashiers *should* always be friendly. I *cannot stand it* when they are rude and insensitive.

(C) I am *angry*.

(D) Is it true that people must be friendly to me? Is it true that I have to be treated well to find happiness in my own life? Is it true that when people behave against my belief that they are bad and must be damned? Where is the proof for all this stuff I am telling myself?

(E) It is not true that everyone must be friendly to me at all times. People can actually do as they please. I can live with how people behave and I don't have to think that it is the end of the world simply because people are rude. I can be sad and unhappy that people choose to behave this way. I don't have to be angry. I can live peacefully even though people act poorly and against my expectations of them. I am no longer angry. I am sad that people choose to behave poorly toward one another.

(A) My husband criticized me.

(B) Husbands *should never* criticize their wives.

(C) I am *angry* and *afraid*.

(D) Where is the evidence that my husband must behave the way I demand? Is it true that even when I behave badly that my husband must treat me nicely? Where is the evidence that my husband must be perfect in order to be married to me?

(E) If I am going to stay married, it may be a better idea to understand that my husband is imperfect and makes mistakes. I make mistakes too. If we are going to be happy in our lives together, we will both benefit from remembering that we are both imperfect. I can be more forgiving of his imperfectness and he may be more forgiving of mine. I am not longer afraid. I am forgiving.

(A) I failed my test.

(B) I *shouldn't* fail tests. If I do, *I am stupid*.

(C) I am *afraid*.

(D) How have I determined that failing is a sign that I entirely a failure? Is it true that if I am not good at everything I do that I am not good? Is it true that when I fail I should be damned? Is it true that I should succeed at everything I do?

(E) If I fail a test, that does not mean I am a failure. I succeed at a number of things that would defy that logic. It really means I failed the test. I can study harder next time. I can ask for extra help. I can resolve that I am not very talented in this area. I don't have to be talented in everything I attempt. I can be happy in my life if I fail. It would be more fun if I succeeded. But people do fail and I am probably likely to fail at something again in the future. It doesn't help for me to berate myself every time I do that. I think I can be more realistic about what failure means. I am no longer afraid. I am motivated!

It is quite possible to go from anger to sadness, anger to forgiveness, anger to LESS ANGER! It all lies in how you perceive and reason.

***

Your potential to create your own emotional consequence is the gold standard for emotional maturity. It will come as you build your skill at identifying and confronting your irrational beliefs and replacing them with rational ones.

***

An Activating Event (A) will evoke a Belief (B) which evokes an Emotional Consequence (C) when divided by Disputation (D) will bring about an Emotional Evolution (E). In other words: $A + B = C / D = E$

***

If you're looking for a classroom, somewhere to practice your ABCs, to have an *in vivo* emotional evolution, look no further than your windshield. There is no better place to encounter the free will and the spirit others can bring to their lives, at the expense of your own, than when we are in our cars. Through the windshield of your car, you can be alone with your thoughts and breathe in the challenges to the emotional balance unfolding before you.

Most of us have an emotional response to people who travel the highway in the passing lane, the left lane, oblivious to those behind them who want to pass.

You're not supposed to be in this lane!

Don't you know the rules?

You should be damned for traveling in the passing lane!

Everyone knows the rules. Why don't you?

I'll show you.

I'll tailgate you until you submit to my superior driving intellect and my authority!

With a clear path to pass on the right, many of us will stay firmly affixed to the bumper of the guy in front of us, determined to teach him how to *follow the rules.* If the car moves to the right and allows us to pass, we feel vindicated for being treated in such an ill-mannered fashion.

(We might give a scolding glance as we pass.)

If the car doesn't move, we will continue to tell ourselves that the *ruthless villain* (idiot, asshole) should behave more courteously, lawfully, considerately and thoughtfully. This emotional mess will continue for a while, until someone gets bored and makes a move to resolve it. Often it is you who will simply decide to pass on the right.

What an idiot!

What a complete asshole!

He's not following the rules.

I hope he crashes into a tree!

That'll teach 'em!

This analogy can be easily applied to your daily, non-driving emotional challenges. When you have a difference of opinion; when people treat you poorly or with disrespect; when others won't cooperate with what you believe they should be doing, you have a choice. You can tailgate them until they change their view, making yourself miserable in the process. You can make yourself unhappy, intent on being inflexible and stubborn, or you can pass on the right. You can smile and wave on your way by, and you can thank them for the lesson they provided you.

You- hoo! Thank you for the learning opportunity!

It's all up to you.

***

I try to relate the experiences in my own personal life to how I explain emotional intelligence (EI) theory. I have concluded that the more real-world knowledge I can offer, the more mutually beneficial my relationship with my readers might become.

I am a firm believer that familiarity breeds *competence*. Let's return to driving. Most days, I set off in my car. I don't wear a seat belt. In fact, I am quite intent against seat belts. I don't like how they feel. I find them confining. Instead, I freely arrange myself in my seat, turn on NPR, take a deep breath and embark on my commute. I am well-prepared for anyone who would intentionally or unintentionally interfere with me.

I almost never use a turn signal and I only half-yield at yield signs and only half-stop at stop signs. (I can tell if the coast is clear when I am approaching these signs, so there is really no need to stop or yield, completely.) If I stop to turn right on red, I normally stop in the cross walk – or in the middle of an intersection when the traffic is heavy. When I am well-merged and soaring toward my destination, I read and send texts, make telephone calls, drive over the speed limit and check what's left of my hair in the visor mirror. Oh, for the record, I never shout at pedestrians or other motorists (like my sister does) and I most certainly would never use hand gestures to emphasize or articulate my position. But, most of the time, I don't really believe the rules of driving apply to me. I am a smart person, and a very safe driver - without having to pay strict attention to the rules. Unlike those for whom the rules were correctly and most competently written, it is my burden, instead, to endure the idiocy of other motorists, each of whom would most assuredly benefit from a driving lesson from me. To cope with it all, I talk to myself.

You feckin' idiot! What in hell are you doing! How dare you do that to me! You are rude and I cannot have that! You will pay for that move, my friend.

ONLY when I am provoked, and my fight-or-flight (stress) response is activated, will my mind override my limbs and I suddenly find myself assertively posturing my shiny ego car against the recklessness and stupidity of others, maneuvering in such a way as to register my displeasure.

In all fairness, I wouldn't dream of using my horn for anything except to provide a little nudge when someone in front of me is too slow to respond to a green light. A toot, if you will - a matter of doing my part to maintain the even flow of traffic.

Driving here and there, up and down, to and fro, is all a straightforward matter of teamwork and cooperation. Without teamwork and cooperation, there is chaos and confusion. Chaos and confusion, when left unchecked, leads to destruction! People who don't cooperate, therefore, must be ridiculed, taunted, nudged and punished – never forgiven. Except if they agree to cooperate. In which case, they are deemed to be good and not bad – like me.

(If I encountered anyone on the road who drove like I do, I would damn them!)

***

I am not a fan of measuring emotional intelligence with anything but one's own individual desire to improve. Emotional intelligence, like most reasonable things, is acquiring a commercial edge. You can be tested for your level of emotional intelligence - for a price. Your level of emotional intelligence, however, is really up to you to decide. If you think you could profit from examining your emotional intelligence, so be it. Weighing up the manner in which I take to road may serves as the impetus for gauging my own emotional intelligence. Your own driving habits may tell you a lot about your own. What can our driving personalities tell us about ourselves? First, you might pay close attention to your thoughts and behaviors while behind the wheel. You may come away with some rather good ideas.

How do you reconcile a disagreement with another driver?

How do you accommodate drivers who you believe are being discourteous?

How well do you follow the rules that you think everyone else should follow?

How are you at conforming to impediments in the road, stop signs, traffic jams, yellow lights, yield signs and pedestrians?

Have your driving habits become patterns, perfect necessities for your continued happiness?

You may find that your answers to these questions will closely approximate how well you regulate your behavior in your walking life. Driving just gives you a chance to see who you really are (and how others perceive you) all in once glance.

Are you willing to express patience, tolerance or pity for those you encounter who disagree with you, impede your way or behave counter to your expectations?

When people make errors that affect your walking life, are you quick to label them bad, wicked, evil or depraved?

Do you provide yourself with enough evidence to determine that someone is inferior, purely on the basis of one or more of the poor choices they've made?

When people act objectionably, do you reconcile yourself by conjuring in your own mind their true intention?

Do you ask?

Even though you have no real way of confirming your suspicions, do you behave as if they were facts?

Do you often feel so morally right that you are willing to claw someone's eyes out to prove it?

Your driving life is replete with parallels with your walking life. Go for a drive. Find a congested area. If you like how you behave, so be it. If you don't, you can change it.

Imagine greater.

***

I received an email from a friend looking for help with a passing-lane problem. He said he wasn't going to give in. He was going to stick to his guns and be stubborn. It was *a matter of principle*, he said. By doing so, he would be losing his partner and everything they had worked together to build for twenty years. But he wouldn't give in because he was right and his partner was wrong and there was no middle ground! He was tailgating.

I'm not going to show that I am weak. I'm going to teach him the rules. If I have to lose everything, I will. It's that important to me.

Helping my friend pass on the right was my goal.

What would it mean if you gave in?

Well, it would mean I am weak.

What would it mean if you were weak?

It would mean people could roll over me when they wanted to.

And if they did that?

That would mean people would laugh at me behind my back, and call me a flunky.

What if they did that?

They would think I was stupid.

Are you stupid?

Not by a long shot.

But if people thought you were stupid, you would be stupid?

I guess.

How can we change that?

I can stop connecting my intelligence with what others think of it.

Yes! And you can pass on the right.

STRATEGY TEN

Sucking the Lemon

Visualize yourself standing in a grove of lemon trees, green, thick branches lined with thorns and smooth, shiny leaves. Hanging from the branches are clusters of perfectly shaped lemons, yellow ovals filled with seeds, juice and pulp. Focus your attention on the most wonderful lemon of them all, grouped among the smaller, less developed ones. Standing beneath the tree, you reach your hand up to pluck it from its place on the branch. As you pull it free, the limb snaps back and regains its original position.

As you gaze at the lemon, sitting in the palm of your hand, feel its weight. Toss it in the air and let it land back in your palm. Roll your hand over its skin and feel its texture, the way it slides over your fingers. Raise the lemon to your nose and inhale its aroma, its scent, its freshness.

Breathe in deeply.

When you're finished, place the lemon on a nearby rock and slice it in half with your pocket knife.

Notice as the juice rolls out, puddles beneath it.

Cut the lemon into wedges.

Raise one of the wedges to your mouth.

Draw your tongue across its flesh.

Bite into it and chew.

You contort your mouth, cheeks, forehead to accommodate the bitter, sour flavor. Your taste buds feel like a puddle of water after a stone has been dropped into it.

***

In basic terms, it is possible to experience the taste of a tart, sour lemon simply by imagining it. That's what I was thinking the day I had my first emotional intelligence Ah-ha! moment. I figured if I were able to imagine the taste of the lemon, I could use my brain for so many more imaginative and sensual experiences.

Your potential for recalling tastes, odors and sensations and feelings lies within the strength of your imagination. You might recollect the taste of mint, bacon, Cheerios, McDonald's, even water. The human brain is a remarkable organ, capable of extracting sensory information from thought, allowing us to go beyond the classical five senses into another realm. This sensory experience depends on recall to replicate sensory signals that simulate the actual corporeal event.

Your brain may first recall an experience you may have had with a lemon, then recall its taste, then recall how your mouth reacted and finally how your body shook, your face convulsed and your mouth spasmed. Each of these pockets of sensory memory, gathered together, create your response to the thoughts of an imagined lemon. If you've never tasted a lemon, or lemon flavoring, you are unlikely to simulate its taste with your mind alone.

***

In very much the same way as we imagine taste, we can imagine emotion and feeling (and stimulate with our minds a biochemical reaction). For example, a convincing actor must recreate fear, anger, sadness and any number of other emotions found among humans simply by recalling experiences with those emotions. The more convincing the actor, the more his emotion resembles real life.

How will I cry on cue?

Just imagine when you were really, really unhappy. Like an actor playing in a scene on stage, your emotions are made to order. To express emotion, you must recall an experience with it. Then you must recall your lines. Then you must assume the role. Your boss criticized you; you take on the role of the worthless employee. Your partner doesn't love you anymore; you take on the role of the entirely unlovable person. The mind can initiate a chemical response to thought, just as if the event were actually taking place. So, if you think you're being treated intolerably, you will take on the role, repeat the script and your body will respond as if you were in an intolerable situation by sending chemical messages throughout your body to help you fight the source of your discomfort.

Imagine that!

Your mind and body work together to protect you. If you tell yourself that you are in danger, your body will prepare you for that. Just as thought of the lemon instigated your taste buds to pucker and your mouth to salivate at the thought of the lemon, assuming the role and recalling the script of a person in peril will release hormones like adrenalin and cortisol into your bloodstream and bring you to a hyper-aroused state.

STRATEGY ELEVEN

Eating the Jelly Bean

Imagine a bowl of brightly colored jelly beans; yellow, green, red. Let the colors and flavors flood your imagination. Which one will you choose? Dipping your fingers into the middle of the bowl, you feel their shiny surfaces pass over your fingernails. You study them, scanning the colors for flavors you don't care for. Goodness forbid you should get a hot cinnamon one. You pop a few into your mouth. The beads of sugarcoated flavor begin to melt, as your saliva washes over them. Bite into the hard shells and allow the sweet flavors to run together. Cherry, tangerine, lemon, green apple, grape and licorice wash over your tongue and down your throat.

Cinnamon!

A suggestion of cinnamon begins to invade your mouth, first by nipping at the tip and sides of your tongue, distorting the taste of the other jelly beans. Your tongue sizzles as the flavor starts to overwhelm your senses, searing your tongue and cheeks with a bite only red hot cinnamon can induce. The flavor is inescapable. The red bean is seemingly toxic, mouth-burning, incapacitating to your taste buds. You chew quickly, the sugar granules grating your teeth like particles of sand. The soft chewy center bursts with juice and sets your saliva on fire.

***

At a time in the distant past, humans depended on a nature-given, automatic response to help reconcile very real menaces to life and limb. Nature allowed for the use of fact and the *fictions* of perception to maximize our response time to threat. We don't actually make an agreement with our bodies to prepare for real or imagined hostility. Our stressful *thoughts* are sufficient to initiate that response.

Much like our imagination can conjure the taste and sensation of a sucking the juice from a lemon or crunching into a cinnamon jelly bean, our perception of other imagined stimuli initiates a sequence of chemical events that depend on thought to activate our protective stress response – our fight or flight response.

Perceiving danger (much like perceiving the taste of a lemon or a fire-hot jellybean), even when no real danger exists anywhere but in our minds, activates a neurochemical, hormonal response that allows us to run faster, jump higher and fight harder than we had ever expected. In today's world, however, threats from attacking bears and lions have been replaced by rude and unfriendly people, the culture of employment, money and family stress. Those kinds of hazards are ever-present in the lives of most people, resulting in what was once a life-saving response, intended to take seconds, now lasting the length of a full day, a week and even years.

The extended secretion of stress hormones that can be initiated through thought alone can have an impact on the integrity of your major organs. Increased heart rate, blood pressure and respiration can result, among other things, in hypertension, obesity and heart disease. It appears that Nature's intention to protect man from harm using perception alone may now be inhibiting our survival.

Our brains are the precious containers of our emotional lives. The fundamental use of emotion may be to help us avoid danger and maximize safety and reward. Your brain facilitates emotion often using *perception* (thinking) alone – regulating hormones, neurochemicals, the pituitary gland, body temperature, the adrenal glands and many other vital activities to accommodate your perception. Much like perceiving the taste of a lemon and a cinnamon jellybean activates a chemical response in your mouth, perceiving threat activates a chemical response in your body.

Perception is guided by experience.

Emotions are guided by thought.

Without *experience, perception* and *thought*, you would not express emotion.

Explaining love, attachment and belonging may not be as much fun as getting a Valentine's Day card, giving a hug or getting a kiss. Suffice it to say, however, we can exist in a world where both interpretations can be accommodated.

It will take the force of will to make that accommodation.

STRATEGY TWELVE

Sucking the Lemon / Tasting a Jelly Bean

We return to the lemon, yellow, plump with juice. Let us imagine that the lemon, this time, is sitting in the refrigerator, cool and ready to be squeezed. You take the lemon from the refrigerator, feeling the coolness of its skin on your fingers. At the sink, you turn on the faucet and run water over the lemon, gently washing it with your fingers.

The water beads up on the lemon's skin.

You place the lemon on the wooden cutting board and watch as the water from the kitchen faucet settles beneath it. You take a stainless steel knife and draw the sharp edge over the lemon, slicing it precisely through its middle. The juice seeps out and mixes with the water beneath each half. You can see the seeds sitting on the surface of the fruit.

Raise one of the wedges to your mouth.

Draw your tongue across its flesh.

Bite into it and chew.

You are chewing a lemon, but the suggestion of cinnamon begins to invade your mouth. Your tongue sizzles as the flavor starts to overwhelm your senses, searing your tongue and cheeks with a bite only red hot cinnamon can induce.

The flavor is inescapable.

You take the lemon out of your mouth and look at it.

Is this a lemon or a jelly bean? It sure looks like a lemon, but it tastes like a cinnamon jelly bean.

You return the wedge to your mouth.

The red bean is seemingly toxic, mouth-burning, incapacitating to your taste buds. You chew quickly, the sugar granules grating your teeth like particles of sand. The soft chewy center, bursts with juice and sets your saliva on fire.

***

Exchanging the taste of the lemon with the taste of cinnamon is similar to *exchanging one emotional response for another.* It is tough to imagine two independent tastes simultaneously.

Your old beliefs are the lemons. Your new ones are the jelly beans. Getting your old beliefs to taste less like lemon and more like jelly beans will present you with a number of sensory challenges.

***

It is likely that you have not developed a pathway in your brain between the taste of a lemon and the taste of a cinnamon jelly bean. It is also likely that you have not developed a pathway from the act of being *insulted* (A) to the emotional consequence (C) of *forgiveness.* There is, however, a well-worn path, instead, to anger and frustration (C).

Building a new pathway, one that provides more opportunity for emotional balance, will likely result in improved emotional intelligence. Doing that will be like sucking a lemon and tasting a cinnamon jelly bean.

If you are angry, you are not likely to express forgiveness or sadness, without first stopping and making an effort to change your thinking.

You are an idiot!

Why you! I should kick you in the throat!

Bring it.

But I won't, because I am going to feel sad for you instead.

What?

Yeah, you apparently have some sort of emotional handicap. I can't be mad at handicapped people. I'd rather forgive you and feel sad for you.

Presently, it is unlikely that you have established a pathway connecting your experience with rudeness to your feelings of understanding and forgiveness. There is a well-worn pathway, however, between being treated rudely and being angry. In order to increase your emotional intelligence however, it is time that you begin to recognize that you can establish new pathways to new emotional responses. Like a path through the woods, it will take time to establish.

I am not getting what I want; I can survive and still be happy in my life.

You are behaving badly toward me; I won't be angry. I will try to understand, instead.

You think I am fat; well I probably am fat. Thank you for noticing me.

Your thoughts and your emotions are under your control.

Bite into a lemon, taste a cinnamon jelly bean – experience insult - express forgiveness. Your emotions are a result of your perceptions. No event has inherent meaning. An event only has the meaning we apply to it.

***

Your brain is the storage center for your emotional memory. And, with a little effort, you could probably conjure anger, sadness, fear and disrespect on cue. You depend on organized patterns of thought to engage with the world and to guide you in your emotional decision making. Your mind consists of structured clusters of experiences and ideas, embedded through time and familiarity. So you are likely to reject emotional information that contradicts your belief. I am reminded of a couple I met with several years ago,

> *I hate it when she takes a sip of my Coke.*
>
> *What about that concerns you?*
>
> *It's nasty. It leaves germs.*
>
> *Aren't you married?*
>
> *Yes, fifteen years.*
>
> *Do you kiss? Do you have sex?*
>
> *Yes, but I was raised not to let people sip from my Coke can.*

People are capable of immense growth, but have a tendency to remain unchanged, even in the face of contradictory information. Unless provoked, people will normally rely on automatic thought processing, rather than careful thinking, to make sense of the world around them. Essentially, people do what they did last time if it worked, inhibiting the influence of new information, giving rise to biased preconception. It is unlikely that you have an area of your brain dedicated to biting into a lemon and tasting a cinnamon jellybean or feeling anger and expressing sadness. In order to accomplish that task, you will have to build a working, mental model of that experience. Growing emotionally means doing very much the same thing. You can express forgiveness when you are treated contrary to your honorable beliefs.

> You can suck a lemon and taste a jellybean.
>
> You can express unhappiness, rather than anger.
>
> It will take the force of will to do that.

STRATEGY THIRTEEN

People are so inconsiderate

Your emotions are made according to your specifications. You create them; so you can un-create them. I recall hearing a story about a man on an elevator. It seems the man, facing a packed lift, entered, turned his back to the other passengers and innocently watched as the floor numbers rolled past, overhead.

As the man stood, waiting to arrive at his floor, he felt a sharp object stabbing into his shoulder blade. He was disturbed, grumbled and moved a bit to the right to escape the jabbing object. The object, however, found its way back under his shoulder blade, and the man grew angrier, placing him off balance, pumping adrenaline into his bloodstream, preparing him for hostility: *People are so inconsiderate. People should be more considerate. Inconsiderate people must be told that they are worthless, because they are inconsiderate!*

As the elevator approached his floor, he told himself that when the elevator door opened he would turn and give the perpetrator a piece of his mind. *How dare he stick his umbrella in my back! The bastard is going to get a piece of my mind, for sure.*

The door opened to the man's floor and, as he was about to step out, he turned to address the man behind him. Preparing his words, he stood face-to-face with a blind woman, holding a cardboard box, a ruler protruding from its corner. In an instant, his feelings of anger turned to sadness and guilt, "*Ummmmm . . . have a nice day,*" he heard himself say. He hung his head and backed out of the elevator.

***

If the condition for your happiness is based on how others behave, you are likely to be unhappy quite often. You can evolve your emotion from anger to any number of other more manageable emotions simply by thinking and perceiving differently. And you can be happy, even when people make emotional and behavioral choices that are contrary to your own. Your emotional response to any event is dependent on how you *perceive* it. To begin to expand your emotional intelligence, you will have to own your own emotions, know that they come from you and your own thinking, rather than placing their origin on others.

I made myself mad by what I told myself. I pissed myself off when I didn't get my own way. I can tell myself something more reasonable, if I want to feel differently.

$A + B = C / D = E$

***

There is an element of *selfishness* in considering only your own perspective in any disagreement.

He shouldn't talk to me that way!
She looked at me with that look and she should watch her face!
She needs to stop doing that or I am going to kill her!

Recognizing and accepting that people have a perfect, inalienable right to choose to act foolishly and irresponsibly will go a long way to improving emotional intelligence.

All day long, people make poor emotional and behavioral choices. Remember, laws don't prevent foolishness; laws establish the consequences. You have a right to make foolish decisions, and you exercise that right from time to time. Not to allow others their perfect right to make poor choices is, well, *selfish*. You make yourself angry by perceiving *selfishly*, interpreting *selfishly* and emoting *selfishly*. It is quite selfish to demand that people act not according their own standard but, instead, *your ideal standard*.

Take a fuller perspective.

Consider your own human potential for making poor choices.

Try applying the consequences you hope for from others when you make a poor choice.

* * *

You've been thinking and behaving the same way for most of your life. You are inclined to place people and things that do not fit your ideal standard of their behavior into a category of *bad*, rather than to consider the possibility that their *choice was contradictory to yours*. You have more than one option available to you for how you can respond to it.

It will take the force of will to do this.

STRATEGY FOURTEEN

Self-Esteem

My blog (http://www.eitheory.com) provides me with daily statistics to help determine my readers' interests – a graphic representation of my reader's enthusiasm for what I write about. During the year I can predict when my readers' interest lies elsewhere, e.g., holidays, warm days, national celebrations, you name it – my readers are elsewhere. If people have time off, they don't normally spend it with my blog. On those days, I could write a detailed map leading to Blackbeard's loot and not even a pirate would bother to investigate. Regardless, I was astonished recently to find a true treasure trove of my own, hidden in my trendy WordPress numbers. It seems each time I write about *self-esteem* there is a colossal spike of interest. I'm intrigued and so, we shall make Strategy Fourteen all about the dreadful topic of self-esteem.

****

To question the unparalleled value of the concept of self esteem on emotional health borders on blasphemy. It is my best judgment, however, that the modern-day idea of self-esteem has been grossly distorted, socially mismanaged and left entirely unregulated. That said it may be that my readers' heightened interest in the topic be the way I try to wring the life from it whenever I talk about it.

Regardless, where there is interest, I shall pursue it.

Shall we?

The term *self-esteem* has lost its original meaning. I find the same phenomenon has occurred with the word *gender*, which has somehow come to mean the same things as *biological sex*. The word *gender* was never intended to have such a strong connection to the word *sex*. The word gender was, however, intended to describe a *psychological mindset* defining one's notion of *masculinity* and *femininity*. The word gender is now used to avoid the word *sex*, altogether, replaced with the word *gender* which is, apparently, more delicate–sounding. The problem is the mismanagement of the word *gender* has entirely distorted the word's use in its original context. Like the words sex and gender, *self-esteem* has become like a paste, or a layer of concrete, used not to enlighten us, but to protect us from something we don't like – something we think of as distasteful.

The term *self-esteem* may be our way to defending against being viewed as average, less talented than someone else. We live in a world that stresses perfection and flawlessness in everyone. Everyone gets a trophy because everyone is a winner! No one can be average or imperfect. Personally, I am more inclined to weigh my own human value using less of a buffer and a bit more clarity.

Well then.

***

When the imaginative concept of self-esteem was first introduced to the world in the early to mid 1960s, people benefited a great deal from it. The term was intended to celebrate the revolutionary idea that humans are an amalgamation of flawed, less flawed and nearly flawless characteristics. Where prior to the concept of self-esteem our personal rating system was held against the strict, singular standard of success and failure, perfect and imperfect, the self-esteem movement offered an alternative to labeling oneself the sum total of our most recent failings. The idea that we could be a combination of traits, good and not so good, all at the same time, was revolutionary! People, it seems, as long as they lived, according to the *original* idea of self-esteem, were each works in progress and, therefore, wholly unratable – especially where children were concerned.

We should have stayed there.

Our modern use of the term self-esteem is not only utterly hopeless in its regard for children, it is at odds with a number of other widely held, entwined social constructs. For example, parenting, for the most part, is a system of teaching children right from wrong, good from bad, best from better. Children are supported in these lessons through appraisal and the subjective opinion of ostensibly knowledgeable adults.

Am I good?

Yes dear. You're a good, good boy!

She didn't play as good as I did.

Yes dear. She's a bad, bad girl.

Yes. She is bad and I am good.

Stay good dear. I don't manage well when you're bad.

I will. I promise.

As children grow and learn, their audience grows larger and includes, among others, teachers and peers. Adolescence and young adulthood is a period of judging oneself against an often harshly narrow social standard. Adolescents respond, as expected, by assessing their social competence against an externally driven appraisal system that is limited to either good or bad. Why not? During childhood, there is very rarely a single moment in the child's social education dedicated to developing anything but an external focus for their personal value.

Everyone says I'm fat and stupid and lazy.

Oh that's not true. You have a pretty face. You are also good at cheese carving. You just need to boost your self-esteem. Let's make a list. You're just going to have to learn to stop listening to everyone. What matters most is how YOU see yourself. Ignore everything else!

This period of early human development is the start of the life-long struggle that most of us continue to experience every day. We are not trained by the adults to manage our personal value. We are trained from the moment of our birth to develop and use an external system of personal measurement based on the opinion of others. That opinion is usually restricted to either good or bad.

You are bad! You cannot behave that way!

You are so good. Good, good, good.

Here lies the foundation for my idea that the original, very innovative concept of self-esteem has been bastardized. Instead of learning to judge our own value, from the start, using more objective, balanced measures, we are, instead, trained early to accept an holistic rating of our goodness or badness from an external, unreliable source – our parents, relatives, friends and neighbors. When we reach adolescence, for example, we have spent the first twelve to fifteen years of our lives receiving global ratings from caregivers, parents, relatives and teachers. One day, when our peers begin to criticize our value, we are asked to ignore their opinion and begin to evaluate ourselves using more objective terms. Suddenly we are expected to manifest some innate ability that will result in our having good self-esteem, without external input. Out of the blue, after years of contradictory training, we must begin to think about ourselves FOR ourselves.   Not only that but, after a lifetime of being *entirely good* one minute and *entirely bad another*, in order to have good self-esteem, we must begin to view ourselves as perfectly good all the time in the face of clearly contradictory evidence. It's no wonder that the biggest issue today in mental health is the concept of self esteem. We are raised to live like a bunch of free-range nut-heads.

In truth, each of us holds within us a psychological and genetic makeup that is a mixture of strengths and weaknesses. And so, we are left with no alternative but to abandon this out-of-date idea of self-esteem and replace it with the more modern concept of *self- and other-acceptance.* We might begin our own journey by telling ourselves, "I can accept myself even though I am not perfect, good, better or best. And, because I can accept myself as imperfect, I can accept that you are not perfect either!"

It will take the strength of will to do this.

***

The prevailing opinion is that in order to have *good* self esteem, we have to reject any value of ourselves that does not meet or exceed *good.* We have to view ourselves as beautiful, intelligent, witty, popular, successful, and talented and, when there is a contrary opinion, misjudged and a victim of jealousy. The fact is some of us are not beautiful, intelligent, witty, popular or successful to any substantial or extraordinary measure. On the contrary, most of us are rather average, while some of us are not average. Some of us are quite intelligent, some of us are not. Some of us are born wealthy, some of us make our wealth and some of us live an average, middle-class life. Some of us are poor. All of us, however, regardless of talent, are intrinsically valuable, because we are human. Self-esteem, therefore, may be made more stable by accepting ourselves as human, along with and in spite of our strengths and weaknesses, *unconditionally.*

Our many attributes, both good and bad, are spread across a spectrum, resulting in *the reality of who we are*. To ignore our weaknesses is to ignore the full spectrum of ourselves. Because we are human, we cannot maintain a rating of perfect goodness. To do so would require building a wall of denial around ourselves, separating our strengths from our weaknesses, struggling daily to conceal our imperfections from ourselves and others.

J.M. Barrie, the author of Peter Pan, illustrates this point: *"Tink was not all bad: or, rather, she was all bad just now, but, on the other hand, sometimes she was all good. Fairies have to be one thing or the other, because being so small they unfortunately have room for one feeling only at a time. They are, however, allowed to change; only it must be a complete change."*

***

Fortunately, people, if they try, can live quite peacefully with their good and bad points. It may be best to begin by accepting that in ourselves that we hold the potential to be ineffective, victorious, unsuccessful, win, fall short, lose, achieve and outright flop. It is a foreseeable inevitability. It may be best to prepare for it.

***

The truth is, ratings of *good* and *bad* are no more than opinions. Opinions are not often under our control, unless they are our own. If you base your value on external sources, your value will always be based on opinion and subject to constant change. The secret to self esteem, therefore, is to *harmoniously coexist with all sorts of opinions* of you, your own and those that are contrary to your own. Opinions can serve to give you information. They cannot, however, serve the purpose of making you entirely good or bad.

Only you can do that.

***

I have concluded that the modern-day concept of self esteem is irredeemable. The concept of self-esteem has spent so much time under foot that it has lost all of its intended meaning. Time, it seems, is better spent viewing our imperfect reflections and embracing them, rather than avoiding and denying them, rating ourselves as good or bad because of them.

***

Unconditional self and *other acceptance* might replace the concept of self esteem one day. The idea of self acceptance, unlike self esteem, cannot come from anything outside of you. It must come from the way you think about yourself, by logically and rationally recognizing your strengths and weaknesses and accepting them for exactly what they are.

Unconditional self and other acceptance will be achieved through logical, balanced and honest *self reflection*, rather than relying on others to give you value based entirely on their opinion of your goodness or badness.

Your appraisal of yourself might be one of stability and self justice. If you plan to make yourself healthier and happier, you cannot allow your emotional, spiritual and intellectual identity to become the possessions of the people around you.

It will take the force of will to overcome it.

STRATEGY FIFTEEN

Murderer's Row

I remember a little girl in my elementary school. She was always dressed so well, little socks with tatted edges, hair in curls. She stood with the other little girls on the playground of the South Elementary School. She seemed to glow, the sun shining through her hair as she hung from the monkey bars, upside down. My first reaction to girls back then was to throw something at them, a rock, a burr, a cat. The burr I threw at her stuck to her wool, stocking cap. I waited for her to make her move. We were in the midst of what I came to refer to as *emotional turn-taking*. I knew she would cry, and I knew what I would do when she did.

It was all very predictable.

Astonishingly, instead, I watched as she removed her hat, ginger hair falling to her shoulders. She inspected my handiwork, pulled off the burr, smiled at it and handed it back to me. She wasn't happy about what had happened, nor was she angry. She was complacent, smiling a simple yet mysterious smile.

I kept an eye on her.

I noticed that no matter what was happening around her, the little girl kept a smile on her face. I was convinced that she was an alien, or a doll on a shelf that never changed its expression. I was most taken by the contrast between her emotional reaction toward me and the one I had expected. She wasn't afraid of me or my mischievousness.

***

I spent much of sixth grade on *Murderer's Row*, a special place for *active* (bad) children; a row of chairs and desks set aside especially, it seemed, for me. (I was often the only student sitting in the row.) They didn't have anything like attention deficit hyperactivity disorder (ADHD) when I was a kid. Or at least no one knew about it if they did. There was no therapy or drugs or individual education plans. We didn't live in a culture where people were given *subscriptions* to medications rather than *prescriptions*. I was just viewed as an active, vigorous albeit *bad* boy who *needed* reining in. On my second grade report card I am described as *full of zip!* and the *class clown*.

I didn't have a clinical label or a *subscription* to Ritalin. I am eternally grateful for that. In the absence of drugs to keep me in my chair, my teachers relied instead on old-fashioned ingenuity, patience and increased frustration tolerance. And, in the case of Murderer's Row, some misguided creativity.

The girl with the chronic smile sat nearby, always well-pressed, intelligent and content. I was in awe of her. The teachers doted on the little girl, and she always had a star, or a turkey, or an orange pumpkin on her forehead. I, on the other hand, when I wasn't sitting in Murderer's Row, spent the day slumped on a stool behind the piano, (occasionally not even worthy of sitting in Murderer's Row) wondering what sense it made for boys to have eyelids if they couldn't turn them inside out now and then.

I had an Ah-ha! moment.

It dawned on me that if I gave up headlocks, shooting spitballs and turning my eyelids inside out and smiled like the little girl, instead, I could improve my lot in life and the teachers (and maybe even the janitor) would like me and I would finally be GOOD!

So I started smiling.

All the time.

Like the little girl.

I was going to be *good* if it killed me.

My new smile wasn't endearing me to anyone. The lunch lady winced when she served me French fries, reaching her tongs to me as if holding a rattlesnake. At first, Mr. Travis, my teacher and the originator of Murders' Row, did a double take and smiled back at me, confusedly. He checked his tie for gravy stains. If he had to turn his back and write on the board, he looked over his shoulder and checked on me, just in case.

As the days progressed, Mr. Travis seemed to become more suspicious, even edgy, as if I were aiming something at him. Finally, one afternoon, he shouted over at me: *What! What! What's up? Wipe that grin off your face! You're making me nervous.* The little girl smiled at me over her shoulder. I made up my mind then and there that I was destined to be forever bad.

I settled in for a lifetime on Murderer's Row.

***

Why was it that the little girl could smile and energize a room, and when I smiled everyone ran for cover? One morning, just as I stepped off the bus, the little girl handed me a note. I was a little stunned. I had never once spoken to her, nor had I ever had a girl pass me a note. Sure, I got notes from my friends that read, 'Eat shit,' or 'I'll buy your bike,' or 'David wants to fight you after,' but never a note from a girl.

What could it say?

I slipped it into my backpack and waited to read it at lunch.

STRATEGY SIXTEEN

Jump In. Get Wet. Cut a Fart. Be Like Al!

Al (Dr. Albert Ellis, the guy I talked about in the beginning of this book) was a psychologist who, as it turned out, was quite famous. He is the grandfather of cognitive behavioral theory and the father of rational emotive behavior therapy (REBT). Both of these theories were introduced to me early in graduate school.

Who really listens in school?

If graduate school had a Murderer's Row, I would have been sentenced to sit there, too.

But I was in Chicago, watching and listening to Al, hearing him cuss and fart. It dawned on me, observing him from my seat in the third row, that he was a lot like me and that he would have been great company in elementary school.

He had that level of *panache*.

Over the course of that weekend in Chicago, Al shared his bodily gases and unapologetically used cuss words to describe everything from his childhood, his inability early in life to get a date and his precarious physical health. Later, as a newly-minted therapist in eastern Kentucky, I decided that, in order to practice Al's therapy more authentically I would have to say *$%$* as often as he did.

No experience left more of an impression on me than when a man and his wife came in for marriage counseling. Mind you, I was not and am not a marriage counselor. Marriage counseling is a specialty area in counseling that requires a great deal of skill and training. I learned that *fact* the hard way. My attitude at the time, however, was to try anything, if I believed it would help.

To see where things went.

Jump in.

Get wet.

Cut a fart.

Be like Al!

The man was well over six feet tall, died black hair, three piece suit, gold crucifix hanging from a chain over his polyester, blue tie. He clutched a well-worn Bible in front of him. His wife was quite plain, diminutive. Her hair was piled at least a foot in the air, making her seem a bit taller. She stood close to her husband's shoulder, as if relying on its firmness to maintain her balance. There was no sign that there was anything askew in their relationship, until the man said he couldn't abide men looking at his wife in the Kroger store, "It makes me angry." Apparently, that *faux pas* alone brought up the notion of divorce.

I jumped in!

I remember it was tough for me to generate discussion with them, this man and his little woman. If I asked a question, they looked at each other and then back at their laps. I thought, considering their obvious religious convictions and their apparent affinity for one another, the man had some very strong beliefs about other men looking at his wife in the supermarket - beliefs that, apparently, were so strong they would lead him to conclude that divorce was the only option.

I got wet!

I talked about thinking and how we feel when we think. I talked about how we could change our thinking and, by doing so change our emotional reaction to nearly anything. The man said, "I don't want to feel better when men look at my wife."

"How would you like to feel?"

"I would like them to stop doing it."

"Is there anything you can do to stop it?"

"Yeah, we can go our separate ways. I ain't living with that."

"Is there no other solution?"

"Nope, she's the woman. She got to do the shopping."

I tried to stimulate discussion about thinking and perceiving. (Al's therapy endorsed the idea that if we can create emotional events in the therapy session *[in-vivo]*, real-time thoughts, the client would provide more useful information than just relying on h/er memory.) My goal was to encourage the man and the woman to tell me their thoughts related to various words like *home, love, church, and meatloaf. How about the word *$%$*?* I decided to cut a fart! (Well, not really, but you know what I mean.) That went over almost like the time Al farted. The man bristled. "My thoughts is if you say that ag'in, we'll be leavin. Me and her don't talk like that."

"Great! What else do you say to yourself when you hear that word?"

"That's about it, I reckon. That's all I'm thinkin'."

"What about you? Do you find the word *$%$* offensive?"

"I done toll you. I thank you for your time, mister. We wish you a fine day." He stood and ushered his wife to the door.

REBT is easy to practice poorly.

***

Working in eastern Kentucky presented me with many learning opportunities, especially where language and its extraordinary potential to offer adventures in language. I learned that we should never assume we are being understood or that we understand.

I was working as a child protection worker, investigating an allegation of child neglect. The caller stated that the mother of the children wasn't feeding them. When I arrived, I was met at the door by a rotund eight-year-old boy and his equally well-fed sister. I discussed the allegations with the mother. She invited me to inspect the food in her kitchen. I found the cabinets well-stocked and a thirty pound turkey, frozen solid, sitting in the freezer. I reached up and took a can of tomato soup off the shelf. To my surprise, the can was empty. The bottom had been removed, the contents emptied and the can placed back in the cabinet. I reached for a box of cereal, a can of beans, a can of ravioli. Each of the containers was empty.

"I don't get it."

"Well, we eat hot meals at the grocery twiced a day. We use our stamps down there."

"Why do you put these empty containers in your cabinet?"

"For people like you comin' around snoopin' and passin' judgment. Makin' me think I'm a bad momma and a bad person. Takes me a week to get over how bad you people make me feel."

"So, why do you think someone would call social services and report you for not feeding your children?"

"They're jealous of my suit case."

"Your suitcase?"

"Yeah, I got a suit case down at the courthouse and they're just jealous of it."

"I'm sorry. I'm not following."

"I got a suit case. Ain't you never heard of a suit case? From a car wreck. I could get $5,000.00 from my neck. They just jealous."

"Oh, I get it. You have a lawsuit."

"No, honey. I got me a suitcase. Lawyers wears a law suit."

If language is truly emotion, it may be best to be multilingual when teaching emotional intelligence to others.

STRATEGY SEVENTEEN

*How did you come to that *\$\$*ing conclusion?*

That weekend in Chicago when Al farted, there weren't any kitten posters, rainbow pillows or books of poetry like I had seen in the student counseling center at school. Missing were the sweat lodges, bungee jumps and aura readings. In place of all that mysticism were my own thoughts, my anatomy, my personal science, logic and Al. Instead of handing out Kleenex, Al handed out challenging questions.

*How the *\$%\$* have you determined that other people make you feel?*

*Are you under some kind of *\$\$*ing spell?*

*How have you decided that handing over your *\$\$*ing emotional life to other people will help you?*

I was interested in what Al was saying, but I was somehow *\$\$*ing afraid of him.

There came a time after leaving Chicago and Al's peculiar way of expressing himself that it started to sink in. His idea of helping people meant TEACHING them how to THINK and SPEAK more effectively, more rationally. I could expect to spend my life teaching people to hear their own inner language, to learn a new inner language and to practice, practice, practice. Al didn't view mental health intervention as a time for petting people and *making* them *feel* good. Thinking, self-talk was the key to achieving mental health. Emotional wellness could not be found in telling people they were *good* and that other people were *bad*. Mental health couldn't be achieved by buying posters that read: *Happiness often sneaks in through a door you didn't know you left open!* Mental health can only be found in sound, rational self-talk and thought!

This guy.

This Al.

This alien from another planet.

This old curmudgeon, farting and cussing, was talking about how my feelings were MY responsibility and ONLY I could do something about them.

Posters couldn't.

Rainbows couldn't.

Unicorns couldn't.

There were no magic wands.

Mental health was like working out. It was a tough commitment. There were failed starts and new commitments. It required dedication and it was easy to get lazy. I remember telling Al I had a neighbor who cut down my newly-planted hedges with his Weed Eater. I told him how I wanted to kill my neighbor:

"How did you come to that *$$*ing conclusion?"

"I came to it when I saw my new hedges in pieces all over my lawn."

Al asked me what I planned to do about my anger.

"What can I do? He killed my hedges and there is no bringing them back. I guess I will have to stay angry and live with it."

"Your *$$*ing anger will kill you. It may be best to do something about it your anger. You can control that, at least. What do you tell yourself when you think about him cutting down your hedges?"

"I tell myself that he shouldn't have done that."

"What should he have done instead?"

"He should have done the right thing. He should have left them alone."

"What does it mean that he didn't do the right thing?"

"It means he is an asshole."

"He does something contrary to your *$$*ing wishes and he's an asshole? He can only be entirely bad? He can't be anything else? Do his wife, his kids, his mother and father think he's an asshole?"

We explored my neighbor's other dimensions.

Oddly, I wasn't AS angry as I was before I started, "If you are not AS angry, something must have happened," Al groused, "What do you think happened? Tell me more about your thinking. What are you telling yourself now that makes it less bad?"

Al taught me that first I think, and then I feel.

Of course, I was familiar with the mainstay mental health intervention lingo: Empowerment, Body Language, Strength-Based Relationship Building and Active Listening. I wasn't as familiar with this *thinking* stuff. I had been taught that, "The counselor provides the growth-promoting climate, and the client is then free and able to discover and grow." I was hearing, "Your client thinks, so s/he feels! As a therapist you teach your client the connection between thought and emotion. Activating events do not cause emotional consequences. You can't *$$*ing feel emotion unless you think first."

Emotion is SCIENCE!

People are not disturbed by things; they are disturbed by their view of things.

I wrote that down.

I read it ten times.

I said it to my friends and anyone else who would listen.

It would take the force of will (and a lot of practice) to really understand those words and believe them.

STRATEGY EIGHTEEN

Self-talk is most often all we have to work with

Most of us tend to fall into an emotional rut. We will do what we did before (if it worked) and we will keep doing it until it stops working. What we do doesn't have to make sense or bring good results. It just has to be the familiar corollary to what is happening. Our emotional response to noxious events is often reinforced by those around us, because people respond to adversity and misfortune in much the same way.

"I can't believe he said that to me."

"Me neither!"

"What would you have done?"

"I would have done what you did."

"Good, now I don't feel bad about doing that."

"I'm miserable, but it was the *right* thing to do."

There is, in fact, a language of emotion that we share not only between ourselves but also within ourselves. We must not only learn to hear it, but to understand it and control it.

***

When I attended the weekend in Chicago with Al, I learned to my own self talk. Al was always very quick to say, "Yes, but what you telling yourself?"

"I'm telling myself that she shouldn't have treated me that way."

"How can you change the *$$*ing way she treated you?"

"I can't, it happened ten years ago."

"So stop telling yourself things shouldn't be the way they are. They are that way! You can't change the past. You can only change the present. What are you, *$$*ing nuts?"

Simply put, if your happiness depends on changing the past, *you will remain as unchanged as your past is fated to remain.*

It is not necessary to explain the past in order to understand the present. We cannot even be sure that our memories of our past are even accurate or dependable. Emotional intelligence can only be increased when we recognize that the past only influences our present through the way we think about it NOW. What do we say to ourselves today that influences how we think and behave today?

I can't move on until I make sense of the past.

How will that help you move on?

I will have some answers.

How will finding answers in the past help you today?

I won't feel so bad about what happened to me.

Can you feel better without having those answers?

I don't think so.

What if you never get the answers you are looking for?

I guess I'll just stay miserable.

***

We can escape from our past by rejecting the messages we repeat over and over inside our own heads.

I'm not successful with men because my father was abusive.

Is your father still abusive toward you?

No, I'm 43 years old. And he died six years ago.

How is your father involved in your relationships now?

I think about him when I'm on dates.

What do you say to yourself?

I say he shouldn't have treated me that way and he has screwed me up for life.

Does that help you enjoy your date?

We can listen to how we talk to ourselves and question the rationality of our beliefs as they exist in our thinking NOW.

Self-talk is most often all we have to work with.

Your self-talk is the source of your emotions. Change it, learn a new language, and you will change your emotional response to nearly anything.

***

We must learn to accept or overturn our thoughts, based on the rationality of our self talk. And we must explore logic and reason as a sound, balanced emotional option.

The easiest way to reveal your own beliefs about yourself and others may be to pay close attention to how you use the words *should, ought, must, have to* and *need*. Without conscious awareness of what these words imply, they may lead to inflexibility in your emotional options. Turning your inflexible demands into flexible options may result in more opportunity for happiness in your life.

***

It has been previously suggested that less demanding, more flexible beliefs can help increase emotional intelligence by assisting you in achieving a more competent, rational method of processing your thoughts. In addition, emotional intelligence can be cultivated if you work forcefully, persuasively and vigorously against your tendency to think irrationally, using a system of logical, pragmatic evaluation of your self-talk.

It will take the force of will to make this happen.

STRATEGY NINETEEN

We've not formally met, but I'm in control now

There is no escaping emotional hardship. If you're lucky, emotion, in all of its glory, will always be a part of your life. Emotion is what makes us human, gives us drive to succeed, pause for thought.

Art, music and murder depend on it.

No book, technique or person who claims to offer safety from emotional hardship will ever fulfill that promise. You will always have ups and downs, good times and bad. Each time you experience some level of adversity, however, you can view it as a *disaster*, an *impediment* or an *opportunity*. Mental health may not be achieved through perfect balance in your life. We may set our sights instead on maintaining a *reasonable* balance, while expecting that things will sometimes not go our way.

It's up to you.

It has always been up to you.

***

Much of how you respond to life is very much under your control. If you don't approach each day with that confidence, your emotional life may be quite impulsive. But if you know where your emotions live, you can knock on the door and have a chat. The first thing you might say is, "We've not formally met, but I'm in control now."

The experience of emotional hardship is not a time for being impulsive or simply doing what you've always done. It is a time for thinking clearly and planning. That is only possible if you know how your emotions are brought to life and how well you have gotten to know and understand them.

***

Time is an astonishing treatment for emotional difficulties. Do you remember your first love? If you're like most of us, it was a whirlwind, 3.5-day romance, filled with commitments for a life together, FOREVER! Struggling to make ends meet, possibly in a run-down flat. But you were happy! You had your love! No matter what happened, you knew your love would keep the both of you cemented together for life, warm in your mutual embrace.

Then WHAM!

The note, passed in the hall between classes.

No eye contact.

Finis!

Just like that, down the toilet with your life!

The phenomenon of losing the person of your dreams, you believed, was an insurmountable problem unique only to you. Only you and possibly sulky, gloomy poets could appreciate the severity of your pain. You hung a new poster over your bed: *The hunger for love is much more difficult to remove than the hunger for bread.*

And you cried.

Then one day you found yourself free of the burden of pining away your life in your room with your French poodle, and you wondered instead what all the fuss was about. That question became even more perplexing when you showed up at your ten-year high school reunion and saw the object of your love balancing a plate of pasta salad on his belly.

Time.

Time, however, not wasted.

While you were suffering through the loss of your love, you were influencing, building and fine-tuning your emotional vocabulary, having an inner dialogue that was designed to help you cope with future episodes of rejection. The inner dialogue you were having might resemble text messaging with yourself:

> *He broke up with me and I cannot stand it.*
> *Yes, it is horrible.*
> *I don't know how I will make it.*
> *You must be too ugly.*
> *I should get my hair cut.*
> *Your acne was out of control.*
> *Yes, I need to lose 20 pounds.*
> *Then he will wish he didn't break up with you.*
> *I'm going to ask Mom if I can have implants!*
> *You will need those to make him feel like shit.*
> *That is totally a plan!*

Depending on what you attributed the rejection to, you developed an emotional text, *a self-talk dialogue,* representing what you will do next time someone rejects you. Your self-talk became, over time, very logical to you. In the above case, the person associated her appearance with being rejected. We might expect that she will be more likely to try to achieve a perfect appearance to prevent future rejection, based on her self-text-messaging.

***

Just like text messaging, there will always be a trace of the text left somewhere on her internal hard drive. For example, the person in the above dialogue may be attempting to portray a perfect appearance, but there is still a trace of self deprecation in her thoughts. *If I look perfect, I cannot be rejected. If I am rejected I must not have been perfect enough.* Not even shredding will destroy whole text beyond all recovery. Likewise, improving your emotional intelligence will not eliminate any of the emotional texts you now use to address the particular issues you face. You will have to review what you now have stored, and make rational judgments about its value to solving your present emotional difficulties or sustaining your emotional health. You will have to learn to think twice. Your original texts may always be there. They don't, however, have to be the text you use to guide your emotional responses.

You can add new text.

You can think again.

***

As a lecturer, I often tell my audience, to their surprise and amusement, that mental health treatment is best applied to those who are not particularly in need of it. *The best place for happy, content people is in therapy! The therapy couch is NOT a place set aside exclusively for the anxious, depressed or angry!*

Are you happy?

Make an appointment with a therapist.

Think about it.

Have you ever tried to make sense with someone who is in an emotional crisis? Playing old texts over and over? Using the same self talk? Playing the same tapes? It's like when a computer gets a virus and the screen starts rolling thousands of messages across your monitor and you can't shut them off.

Do disturbed people listen to reason?

Do unbalanced people want to actually solve problems?

What, pray tell, could anyone have ever said to help you adjust to losing your first love?

I am a firm believer in strengthening one's coping skills BEFORE those skills are actually needed. The WORST time to prepare for a computer virus is when it is infected.

***

As a culture, we don't adequately prepare our young ones for misfortune and hardship. In fact, we do what we can to shield our children from the unfortunate side of life; making reality even more of a shocker later on.

Prepare!

Emotional adversity will likely to be part of your life until the end of your days. There is no way to escape unhappiness, in all of its emotional forms. We will be better served by preparing for it; building coping skills that will be available when life isn't going as well as we had planned.

STOP! reacting to adversity.

PREPARE for it!

I will be most happy when, somewhere on this planet, a *therapist* says to a client, "What brings you in today?"

"Well, doc, I am as happy as a clam."

"OK, so you have never been happier?"

"You bet'cha!"

"Great! Let's begin."

"I'm ready!"

Remember, we all have problems and we always will. Problems are what keep us human. We are expected to learn how to cope with future problems by experiencing problems now. They are the by-product of living in an imperfect world. Our inner language is what we rely on to help us cope with that unfortunate reality. And it is our inner language that we must focus on strengthening, if we are going to achieve our highest emotional potential.

It will take the force of will to do that.

STRATEGY TWENTY

If I'm wrong, you're stupid

Most of us prefer to be in balance, a time when our biological, psychological and social worlds are all equally composed.

A state of calm.

Equilibrium.

Like a deer grazing in a field, a layer of mist hovering over a still, tranquil pond.

Ducks flying overhead.

Balance.

The distant SNAP! of a twig and the deer suddenly places more weight on *fear* than *calm*.

Imbalance.

Heightened awareness.

The deer freezes, pricks up its ears and tries to make sense of every sight and sound. Signals coming from all directions. Its pupils dilate. Its sense of smell becomes more acute. Its hair stands on end. The intense strength that will be needed to fight or flee begins to gear up. It is the animal's natural response to danger.

You have one much like it.

An innate warning system, triggered not by sound but by thought. Much like the deer, your thoughts are the perception of danger, initiating a sudden burst of neuro-chemicals and hormones intended to sustain your efforts to survive, circulating, priming you for fighting or fleeing. The response might begin with an accelerated heart beat. Inhibition of stomach and upper-intestinal action soon follows. Constriction of blood vessels occurs, along with a release of nutrients for muscle fuel. Dilation of blood vessels for muscles, inhibition of the lacrimal gland and salivation , dilation of pupil, relaxation of bladder, inhibition of erection, auditory exclusion, tunnel vision, acceleration of instantaneous reflexes and shaking constitute many of the automatic responses both animals and humans experience when sensing threat.

***

There is quite a similarity between the deer's reaction to threat and your perception of it. Imagine that you're on the phone with your doctor's office. You have been placed on hold and forgotten. You wait and wait and wait. Finally, the receptionist returns to your call and asks if she can help, "I've been waiting for fifteen minutes." Your heart is beating rapidly. You feel yourself beginning to sweat. You hear, "How can I help you?" You feel yourself beginning to shake, "I already told you I wanted to make an appointment to see the doctor." Your voice rises. You hear, "No need to get angry. Name?" The hair on the back of your neck seems to stand on end. You say, "My name? I already gave you my name!" You hear, "Ma'am, you will have to give me your name again, if you want me to help you." Filled with adrenaline and other protective chemicals, you are now well-prepared to fight, "My name? Oh, my name is Eat Shit!

Yeah, that's my name. Eat Shit and Die is my last name!" You feel your whole body shaking as you slam the phone into its holder. For a few minutes you cannot think clearly or stop shaking. After a few minutes, the chemicals have begun to dissipate, so you call your sister and tell her what happened, "What would you have done? How would you have responded? Was I right?"

***

We have only one natural response to stress, and we use that single response to protect ourselves from all types of threat, both physical and emotional. Nature's gift to protect us from extinction has not adapted well to our contemporary world, I'm afraid. Modern threats are primarily emotional, not often physical. They might include fear of the unknown, inconsiderate people, trying to control destiny, traffic jams, the loss of friends and family, hopelessness.

Our human blueprint cannot make the distinction between physical and *emotional threat.* Ideally, if we are confronted with an emotional issue, we would have an innate system that relied on our intellect to resolve it. But we are programmed to fight, run or freeze when we perceive danger – emotional or physical. Like hearing a twig SNAP! our thoughts over a disagreement with another person (who is perceived as a threat) will prepare our bodies automatically for hostility:

"I have to disagree with you. I think you are wrong."

"If I'm wrong, you're stupid."

"You can't say that to me."

"Sure I can. I just did."

"Why you! I'll show you!"

***

The threats we encounter in our daily lives are menaces to our minds. Much like being attacked by a lion (or a wild and wooly

107

groundhog) judgments of our character are assaults on our values, morals, principles and standards. Slights to our appearance. Snubs about our child's school performance. A slur about our mothers. These are our emotional threats – our twig SNAPS! Each setting off an alarm to protect us from a perceived danger:

May I help you?

I need to return this cleaver.

Do you have a receipt?

No, I lost it.

We don't take returns without a receipt.

It's the wrong size.

I'm sorry I can't help you.

What do you expect me to do with it?!

That's your option. We cannot take it back without a receipt.

It's my option? Are you getting smart with me?

(Staring at each other.)

(Silence)

How about I shove it up your ass? Is that one of my options?

Security!

Luckily, there are alternatives to your emotional responses. It will take the force of will to use them.

STRATEGY TWENTY ONE

Attachment and *Fear*

For survival purposes, people are designed to express two fundamental emotions: *attachment* and *fear*. People are designed to express two fundamental behaviors: *nurturing* and *non-nurturing*. People have one fundamental goal: *balance*.

It may be that we begin life with a built-in capacity to express attachment and fear. *Attachment to ensure cooperation with one another; fear to make certain we have an effective, protective response to threat* and *danger*. Our culture ensures that we acquire a purposeful use of attachment and fear, in order make certain that we cooperate with one another and survive as a species within that particular population and culture.

There are a number of similarities between people in our general, world culture. It is our subcultures, our families, the towns we grew up in, the states we come from, that give us our *unique interpretations* of attachment and fear. We are born with the capacity to attach and to fear. Our unique cultures teach us how to attach and to whom, and who and what to fear.

Our brains begin their journeys through life symbol-ready, wired for learning, extremely receptive to experience for our continued emotional development. A child's early encounters with others, especially home life, have an immense influence on confirming emotional customs and traditions, transforming attachment and fear into the many other dimensions with which we are familiar. We learn from our caregivers which behaviors and emotions contribute to, or inhibit, cooperation and survival.

***

As a culture, we may share many of the same beliefs about behavior. We may have the same expectations of one another, to a large extent. It is our unique exposure to our own inimitable cultures that gives the added color to our personal experiences and our individual expression of emotion.

As a young New-England-born therapist in eastern Kentucky, I was often the focus of attention. Whenever I opened my mouth and my New England accent was detected, I immediately became dubious. People generally assumed people from Massachusetts were rich, snobby, impatient and critical of southerners. The particular area of Massachusetts I come from pronounces many of its words with a somewhat British flair. For example, half is pronounced (haAHf); path (paAHth), bath (baAHth), can't (caHHn't) and, the old stand-by car (CaAHH).

One afternoon, I was working with a very unhappy woman, discussing her continuing relationship with her girlfriend. It seems that she was so overwrought on this particular day she wanted to spend some extra time with me. My policy was to spend forty-five minutes in actual therapy and fifteen minutes talking about what the client heard during the session, "I'm going to have to stay a few more minutes. I'm a mess."

"No, you caHHn't. I have another client. You know our agreement." She drew back in horror, "Is something wrong?"

"You don't have to call me names."

"Names?"

"You called me a cunt. You been doing that since I met you. I'm sick of it."

"What!? I didn't say that."

"That's what I heard."

"Oh, I said caHHn't."

"See! You said it again!"

"Goodness."

STRATEGY TWENTY TWO

You can really push my buttons!

It is not uncommon to hear someone say, "He really knows how to push my buttons," or "I'm just yanking your chain." The implication being that we actually have buttons and chains and they are available for others to push, pull and yank. What exactly do people mean when they say these things? How does believing that you have buttons and chains, on any level, interfere with improving your emotional intelligence?

For the benefit of moving your emotional intelligence into a more manageable realm, let's begin by declaring: YOU HAVE NO BUTTON OR CHAINS! (If you do, you should see a general contractor.)

Of course if you believe you have chains and buttons, you will behave as if you do. The same goes for believing you are Jesus, ugly, important, Sophia Loren, unimportant, beautiful, a genius or a nitwit. If you believe it, you will behave as if it were true. You can believe you have bells and whistles, too. Anything is possible within the confines of your own skull. Likewise, once people find out that you believe (on some basic level) you have bells, horns, buttons, whistles and chains, they will be forever grabbing for them and you will be forever behaving as if they have hold of them. This imaginative process (which is precisely what it is) alone is enough to inhibit or even prohibit the improvement of your emotional intelligence. For that reason, we will have to dismantle this dangerous button. Stomp the life right out of it.

First we have to find it.

***

Locating your button will be tough, because it doesn't exist. You know that, already. But let's imagine that you actually do have a button. What would it look like? What would be inside it? What would make it work?

I think we can all agree, at minimum, that the button would be RED. Of course you can't have your button hanging from your shirt pocket. You might drop it, lose it or someone may push it too hard and break it. So we will place it snuggly inside your skull, for safekeeping.

Imagine that.

When your button is in a resting state, it blinks the words DO NOT TOUCH in large white letters, across its face. When it is pushed, pulled or yanked, it makes a SNAP sound, much like the sound of the twig that snaps in the distant forest and scares the deer. Then it would pulse and swirl, like a police beacon.

***

Now that we know what your button might look and sound like, let's discuss its other features. The most misunderstood characteristic of your button is that others can push it. This is where nearly everyone gets it wrong. Your button, being sealed deep inside your own skull, makes it impossible for others to push it or to even see all of its flashing and whirling.

In the absence of any other logical button pusher, we will have to settle on YOU as the pusher of your own button. After all, your thoughts are the only truly identifiable elements that can reach deep inside your skull, and initiate an emotional response (without surgery, of course). You will have to rely on your perceptions, the electrical impulses generated from your own thinking, to reach your button and push it.

SNAP!

***

Your own thinking pushes your button and sends blood to your face, makes your heart beat faster and your palms and hands sweat and shake. You can't seem to control your facial expressions. The tone of your voice rises:

He has no right to talk to me like that - SNAP!

She should be more respectful of me – SNAP!

She doesn't know how important I am – SNAP!

I worked hard and he should recognize that – SNAP!

***

People seem to impulsively place the power of their button on things outside of themselves. They seem to do the same thing with their emotions. Emotion is too often believed to come from some external source, outside of ourselves: *You make me so angry. He made me sick to my stomach. They are so irritating.* Your button is simply another manifestation of this phenomenon. People don't make you feel. You make yourself feel by what you tell yourself about what people do and say. People don't push your buttons. You push your own buttons; all of it a product of your own mind; a product of your thinking.

If you could take your button apart, you would find it jam packed with rules, laws, expectations, directives, decrees and beliefs about yourself and the world you live in. These imperatives (absolute rights and wrongs) are the life force of your button. These are the thoughts that give emotion substance, keeps it alive:

My husband should always kiss me when he gets home from work. If he doesn't – SNAP!

My boss should always praise me for my hard work. If she doesn't - SNAP!

I should never be misjudged or treated unfairly. If I am - SNAP!

***

When the world within you is going the way you want, when all the absolute imperatives that float around inside your head are being respected by others, you are in balance. People will often do nearly anything to regain emotional balance. You may lash out at those who ridicule you, in order to regain inner balance, to scare away their critical opinion of you. There are methods for improving the odds that you can maintain balance, even when you are ridiculed, criticized and generally don't get what you think you should get. You will first have to get rid of the idea that you have buttons. In order to start the dismantling process, you will have to review your imperatives, the demands you place on others, and turn them into preferences and desires, WANTS rather than NEEDS. You will have to start learning your new language: *I would like it if people didn't ridicule me. If they do, I can adjust and I can continue to live happily. I would like it if people were understanding of my failures. If they aren't, I won't like it, but I can still be happy in my life. I would like it if people were supportive of me. If they aren't, I can still be happy in my life. If people are not understanding and supportive, I certainly can stand it. I can stand a lot of things I don't like. I can be happy if people are not understanding and caring of me. Maybe not as happy as I would if they were, but happy nonetheless.*

***

You have no buttons, chains, horns, bells or whistles. You only have your thoughts. And it is through the management of your thoughts that you will achieve improved emotional intelligence.

It will take the force of will to change it.

STRATEGY TWENTY THREE

I think we are going to be OK

We've explored the idea in previous chapters that each of us is a delicate grouping of biological, psychological and environmental (social) elements, each contributing to our individual the expression of personality. In fact, bio-psycho-social theory is an holistic philosophy of health care that does not endorse the belief that these features can ever be viewed separately. Instead, they work in conjunction with one another. The more closely these components are harmonized, the more physically and emotionally balanced one can expect to be. EI theory appreciates this position, particularly when reflecting on the functional use of personality and its impact on our overall health status.

The psychological constituent of the bio-psycho-social model is believed, generally, to be a product of thinking, evaluation and emotional expression (feelings).

Individual psychology might be defined as a system of turn-taking, a product of our unique experiences with others within our own inimitable cultures. Although the term *turn-taking* is most often used to describe the rules in game-playing, it is also the model we might rely upon to cooperate with one another in our daily, social lives. Turn-taking, in a social context, consists of scripts, subtle signals, facial expressions, voice intonations and pragmatic rules learned over time, shaping our complex social rules and customs. We take turns expressing our thoughts and clarifying our meaning. We impose a level of cooperation and an expectation of collaboration between speakers and listeners. Just as in game-playing, when a player breaks the rules or goes out of turn, the game is disrupted and the other players rebel, calling for a review of the rules in order to regain balance in the game:

You aren't supposed to do that!

Yes, but I want to.

That is totally against the rules. Stop it!

I do it all the time.

Where did you learn that? Where were you raised?

Throughout life we establish, through experience, the general principles of cooperation, congregation and copulation – resulting in a set of social constructs (rules) that start their development at birth and become the frame of reference we use to address most social situations. Social constructs represent meaning – a process of perception and cognitive/social verification. We internalize these rules of engagement, practice them and produce a system of social navigation:

When I do this, you say 'Thank you.'

When I do this, you express anger.

When this happens, you say, 'Excuse me,'

This is what boys do.

This is what girls do.

You are a bad boy! I will let you know when you're a good boy.

You are a good girl, but don't make a mistake because then you will be a bad girl.

– Voila! the creation of our personal rule book.

She did that.

What did you do?

I did this.

I would have done this and that.

So I was wrong to do this?

Yeah, she got over on you. Now you look like an idiot.

Oh shit!

Yeah.

Our rule book is an internal structure, the dialogue we have with ourselves that consists of a complex inner wisdom made up of words, phrases, body language and perspective-taking. If you want to identify the components of your complex inner wisdom, you might begin by identifying the absolute terms you use in your self-talk. Words like *should, ought, must, have to* and *need* represent your standard of normal, your perfect right and your perfect wrong. These are the standards you have learned to expect from others, the standards that, when applied to others, result in countless, repeated experiences with emotional discomfort.

Most of us were trained in an environment of right and wrong, where few alterations were allowed from what should and shouldn't be. It would have been a rare occasion for our social educators (parent, neighbors, relatives, teachers) to say, "Let's talk about the parts of your behavior that were right and the parts that were not right. Then we will compromise based on how they behave in France." Our social educators trained us to behave properly in our own social environment.

Our emotional educators were the sole determiners of the appropriateness of our behavior. Your early behavioral training was always a push toward getting it perfect. And you maintained that perspective throughout your life (whether you're ready to believe that or not). When things are the way they should be, there is balance, a perfect, serene world where everything within your perception happens as it ought to. If your expectations are frustrated, when things are the way we believe they shouldn't be, you will feel some level of upsettedness.

You will begin your emotional downfall by rating yourself and others as perfectly bad or perfectly unfair, and things as magnificently awful for not meeting the ideal standard you set for what should, ought, must, have to and need be. Your search for perfection and the ideal standard represent the emotional struggle within each of us, our neurotic attempt to hold ourselves and others to a benchmark of perfect rightness – excellence. When we apply the word *should* to anyone or anything, we are demanding nothing short of complete perfection from them. That expectation, however honorable, is often undermined by those who do not behave perfectly or ideally and those who are not willing to participate with your expectation of their behavior.

Conflicts in your thinking represent a threat to your mind and produce a fight or flight response that impacts your ability to function healthily.

It will take the force of will to overcome this nut-headed-ness.

STRATEGY TWENTY FOUR

To be in balance

We cannot sustain a state of repose and anxiety at the same time. It would have been an evolutionary calamity to design humans to think about emotional and behavioral choices when faced with a potential life-threatening condition: *That looks like a bear. It seems to be creeping toward me. I wonder what it wants. I think I should run, but I would like to finish picking these blueberries.*

Instead, with little help from internal dialogue, the perception of danger spills adrenaline into our system, promoting heightened alertness. Adrenaline primarily binds to receptors on the heart and heart vessels, increasing heart rate, forcing muscle contraction and increased respiration. Adrenaline allows us, like the deer and the imaginary button, to fuel our muscles and fight or make a mad dash for safety. Once we have annihilated or escaped the threat, we can be expected to begin a process of de-escalating, returning to repose.

This system is indispensible, designed specifically to protect us, permitting a speedy response to acute stressful events. Our ancestors, rather than thinking about the bear and what to do, screamed bloody murder and immediately grabbed something to fend off the potential attacker. Without thinking, they readied for a fight, fueled by a rush of hormones and neurochemicals specifically designed to provide extra strength and endurance.

In addition to the short-term protective response, Nature also provided us with the long-term capacity to maintain heightened awareness, possibly for travel in unsafe territories or between hunting grounds. The hormones needed to maintain this stress response may also have helped during times of famine by aiding in the breakdown of tissue, in order to feed vital organs.

The long-term stress response, although quite adequate thousands of years ago, has not adapted well to our contemporary demands. Our modern stressors are primarily emotional, rarely physical, and not often used for survival. In fact, we would probably live better in our modern world without or with a very limited long-term stress response.

But we only have one stress response, and that one response is used to meet the demands of not only physical threats but emotional ones, as well.

***

On a daily basis, we are inundated with emotional perceptions of danger, however great or small. Our jobs, traffic jams, politicians and the pressures of family life are all potential sources of long-term stress, lasting days, weeks, months – even years. Real problems arise when the systems designed to protect can ultimately harm or even kill us.

It takes a lot of energy to sustain the stress response, short- or long-term. Long-term maintenance of the stress response, however, requires additional substances to meet the extended demand for fuel. Cortisol, a hormone, triggers an increased release of adrenaline, while DHEA (dehydroepiandrosterone) and testosterone decrease. Elevated cortisol levels can result in muscle breakdown, suppressed immune function and increase the risk of illness and injury. Unlike adrenaline, which binds to the heart, cortisol binds to receptors on fat cells, liver and pancreas, increasing glucose levels to fuel muscles. It also sustains the temporary inhibition of digestion, growth, reproduction and the immune system.

***

Although our stress response was designed to make us safe and help us survive, it has become, instead, a menace to our very lives, one of modern man's most distressing paradoxes. Over time, if cortisol stays in our system at high levels, and is not used for the purpose it was intended, it begins to digest bone, muscles and joints. High blood pressure, a compromised immune system and a weakened or damaged heart are additional potential results. While the human body is an amazing thing, with an astounding ability to counterbalance emotional imbalance, nothing we can do using our stress response alone will result in a reduction in these conditions.

***

Each of us has within us, a deep longing for everything to be put right, to be in balance. So our minds and our bodies will actively attempt to cope with emotional challenges, expending the energy necessary to meet that demand. Once the threat to our balance is overcome, we are expected to resume our lives in peace, until the next short-term challenge presents itself. A steady diet of long-term stress, however, without the requisite period of relaxation, places an unusual burden on our capacity to rebound. Nature never intended the stress response to last as long as we sustain it in modern times. We have only one system for responding to threat, and it has not adapted well to our contemporary demands.

This is the cycle in which most of us engage the world.

It will take the force of will to break it.

STRATEGY TWENTY FIVE

I'm not changing my beliefs

In previous chapters we discussed the important link between human biology, psychology and social exposure (bio-psycho-social) and how we communicate emotion. The key factor in all of this (if it can be drawn down to only one strategic factor) is the influence individual *belief* has on the expression of emotion. Our individual *belief systems*, our personal construct for knowing right from wrong, good from bad, evil from virtuous, moral from immoral, when examined properly, can result in overwhelming improvement in our emotional intelligence (EI.

What do you believe to be true? What *should, ought, must, has to* or *needs* to exist in the world in order for you to be in balance - to be content? Are there any exceptions? What happens when the world is not meeting your unwavering demands?

Your beliefs, your current schema for perceiving, thinking and emoting in your social world, hold sway over improvement to your emotional intelligence. Your beliefs trigger those biological responses (otherwise known as the *stress or freeze, fight or flee* response) placing you in the position of solving a precarious physical and emotional puzzle.

I don't like this person's behavior; shall I freeze, fight or flee?

Your beliefs, when challenged by others, trigger a neurochemical-hormonal protective response that can interfere not only with your thinking and reasoning, but your physical health, as well. When you are facing adversity, hardship and misfortune, your brain will react to protect you from it, just as it would protect you from a rampaging emu or a hungry black bear. *Your brain takes what you tell it and determines that there is trouble and you need protection from it.*

It's all quite automatic.

Your brain has a mind of its own.

In order to change this response, making the experiences in your life more manageable, you will have to change what you believe *must, should and ought to be* and still remain content when you don't get your way. You might also examine quite closely what you think you *need* in order to achieve emotional balance.

Make room for error.

I once worked with an employee and his manager to resolve a matter between them.

Your behavior is unprofessional.

What does unprofessional mean?

Don't give me that. You know what I mean. Even the tone of your emails is rude.

How will I know that I am writing something with a bad tone? I don't write tone into my email? I think you read tone into my email.

I guess I will have to tell you when you are being inappropriate.

Sounds good.

That doesn't mean I won't be writing you up after I explain it to you.

Regardless of your individual EI goal, understanding the power of your beliefs, and the impact they have on your behavior, can open up a whole new world of emotional awareness for you. Your first eye-opening experience should be that there is no way for people to know what expectation you have for them unless you tell them and they tell you how willing they are to abide by your social rules. (And even then, as in the above case, that is not enough.)

No matter how much wisdom is gained from knowing where our emotions live, unless you are willing to accept that your way is not the only way, your beliefs are not the only beliefs, and that there are other perspectives to consider, you cannot grow. This is a *necessary truth* in EI theory and will likely lead, if fully appreciated, toward improvement.

Often, people will forcefully, vehemently hold on to their beliefs, even if they result in more anger, depression, isolation and physical illness. It may be that they fear compromise, because compromise may mean that they will have to give up some part of what they believe, leaving them somehow changed.

I will never accept that my son is gay.

But he is gay.

I don't have to accept it.

What other alternative is there? You don't have to accept that it's daylight, but that doesn't make it untrue.

If I accept it, he will think it's OK.

I think he already thinks it's OK.

He can't come around here anymore.

He is still your son.

I'm not changing my beliefs.

Even from the very people who are actually seeking EI improvement, some level of resistance is predictable:

I don't want to think this way anymore. I want to change my beliefs.

How is it a problem for you that your son is gay?

People will make fun of our family.

Anything else?

He won't give me any grandchildren. I wanted grandchildren.

What else?

Someone will hurt him.

And?

I won't know how to act around him, if he brings someone over for dinner.

Anything else?

I'm scared.

Ah, so that's what the problem has been all along?

I think so.

It may be that many of our beliefs are so intimately connected to our other beliefs that to compromise one of them would mean making some adjustment to others.

It will take the force of will to recognize these connections.

STRATEGY TWENTY SIX

Practice

Let's put a little *in vivo* experience behind what we have learned about emotion so far. I chose this particular client because the discourse is fraught with issues of *self esteem* and other disturbing cognitions.

Background: *Elliot* is a white, English-speaking, unmarried 17-year-old high school student. *Elliot* is an only child. He lives with his father, who is an air force chief master sergeant, and his stepmother, who works at the Base Exchange.

Elliot is attending therapy at the request of his stepmother. *Elliot* recently told his father he is gay, and his father responded by shouting at him, slapping him in the face and telling him he was *no longer my son*. *Elliot's* father also told him he was *filthy, an abomination, disgusting, a drug addict, a sex fiend and a pedophile*. He ordered him out of the house and forbade his wife to ever speak with him again.

Elliot went to his room and his father left the home. His father has been away from home for three days. His stepmother is worried the family is collapsing.

***

Session One

Therapist: How can I help you?

Elliot: I told my father I was gay and he slapped me and disowned me.

Therapist: How is that a problem for you?

Elliot: How is a problem? What do you mean, how is it a problem for me? Jesus, how would it be a problem for anyone?

Therapist: I mean just that. How is your father's rejection of you a problem for you?

Elliot: I wasn't expecting that question.

Therapist: Then we are off to a good start. How is it a problem for you?

Elliot: I guess it's a problem for me because I want him to accept me.

Therapist: What does it mean when your father doesn't accept you?

Elliot: This is getting even more confusing.

Therapist: If your father doesn't care for you, what does it mean?

Elliot: It means he doesn't love me.

Therapist: Does it mean anything else?

Elliot: It means he doesn't respect me.

Therapist: Anything else?

Elliot: It means I don't live up to his expectations of me.

Therapist: Anything else?

Elliot: I think that's about it.

Therapist: Let's arrange all this information. You told your father you were gay and he rejected you. You took that to mean he doesn't love you; he doesn't respect you and you are not living up to his expectations. Is that correct?

Elliot: Yes. That's about the size of it.

Therapist: That is what you think.

Elliot: Yes, that is what I think.

Therapist: What are you feeling?

Elliot: I'm pissed. I'm angry.

Therapist: Sometimes when we are feeling anger, we are also feeling fear. What are you afraid of?

Elliot: I'm afraid my father thinks I am a piece of shit.

Therapist: Yes, I can see that. What would it mean if he did?

Elliot: What would it mean? It would mean that I am a piece of shit.

Therapist: Can it mean anything else?

Elliot: No.

Therapist: Your father's opinion seems to have the power to turn you into a piece of shit. Yes, I can understand your fear. You don't look like a piece of shit, but I'll take your word for it.

***

Session Two

Elliot: You're making fun of me.

Therapist: Of course not. But what would it mean if I were?

Elliot: It would mean you don't take me seriously.

Therapist: Of course I do. But what would it mean it I didn't.

Elliot: This is getting like exercise.

Therapist: It is like exercise. It's exercising your mind. Play along. What would it mean if I were not taking you seriously, aside from the waste of my time and your money?

Elliot: I guess it would mean that you think I'm a clown.

Therapist: What if I did think that? What would that mean?

Elliot: I suppose it would mean that I am a joke.

Therapist: You give me a great deal of power.

Elliot: How so?

Therapist: If I decide to not take you seriously, that would make you into a clown?

Elliot: I never thought of it that way. I'm not sure I want to agree with you now that you put it that way.

Therapist: You don't look like a clown, but I can take your word for it.

Elliot: I'm not a clown.

Therapist: OK, you are not a clown, but you are a piece of shit?

Elliot: I guess.

***

Session Three

Therapist: So, you are not a clown, but you are a piece of shit?

Elliot: I don't want to be either.

Therapist: What are we going to do, then?

Elliot: Isn't that your job?

Therapist: I'm not sure. What do you think my job is?

Elliot: To fix me. To tell me what to think.

Therapist: You seem to be doing fine telling yourself what to think.

Elliot: I think I'm dizzy.

Therapist: Let's get back to your father. He doesn't like you to be gay. He has disowned you and shown you disrespect. You believe these events have turned you into a piece of shit. Is that where we are?

Elliot: Yes, I guess.

Therapist: What does a piece of shit feel like?

Elliot: Oh boy. A piece of shit feels like really depressed and really sad and really scared.

Therapist: That doesn't sound at all like how I imagined a piece of shit to feel.

Elliot: I'm not really a piece of shit. It is a figure of speech.

Therapist: Oh, that makes things easier. I was thinking I was going to have to call a plumber.

Elliot: Very funny.

Therapist: So what we really have with us today is *Elliot*, a 24-year-old male who is homosexual and who has been rejected by his father and now feels depressed, sad and scared?

Elliot: That about sums it up.

Therapist: Now we're talking.

***

Session Four

Elliot: I wish I didn't have to be gay. It would make things a lot easier.

Therapist: What about being gay concerns you?

Elliot: Everything.

Therapist: Goodness, what motivates you? I mean, if things would have been a lot easier, what compelled you to tell your father you were gay?

Elliot: I wanted to be honest with him and I wanted him to accept me.

Therapist: What did you imagine being honest and seeking acceptance would bring?

Elliot: Probably exactly what I got.

Therapist: Then why do it?

Elliot: I think it's best to be honest.

Therapist: And accepted?

Elliot: Yes, most of all acceptance. People need acceptance.

Therapist: Do they?

Elliot: Of course they do.

Therapist: What would it mean if people didn't accept you?

Elliot: It means that I am not acceptable - that there is something wrong with me.

Therapist: All that from someone not accepting you?

Elliot: Pretty much.

Therapist: Let me get all this straight. Your father rejects you, and you are a piece of shit? Someone doesn't accept you, and you are unacceptable? That is a lot of power to give to other people. It seems whenever someone thinks something about you, you immediately believe it's true. It's like someone put a spell on you and you become whatever they want you to be. You cannot have happiness in your life unless everyone you meet loves and accepts you?

Elliot: Yes, I suck and you are just telling me how much.

Therapist: So I have that same kind of control over you?

Elliot: Obviously.

***

Session Five

Therapist: It must be tough having to go back and forth between being a piece of shit and being unacceptable. What do you suppose we can do about that?

Elliott: You can make me straight.

Therapist: How do you suppose that would help?

Elliot: People would like me.

Therapist: Goodness, is that all it takes?

Elliot: Yes. If I were straight, I wouldn't have these particular problems.

Therapist: Do you think all of your problems would be solved?

Elliot: Not all of them, but most of them.

Therapist: What about the problems you still have?

Elliot: I could work on those.

Therapist: You would still have problems?

Elliot: Yes, but not these problems.

Therapist: Being straight wouldn't solve all your problems?

Elliot: No, I would just have different problems.

Therapist: How do you suppose we can help you get to the point where you didn't have any problems?

Elliot: I would have to be perfect.

Therapist: If that's the only way you can be happy with yourself, shall we set that as your goal? To be perfect?

Elliot: Not really. I don't think I will ever be perfect. No one's perfect.

Therapist: How do you know that?

Elliot: The odds are you will have some problems or that someone won't like you for some reason that isn't under your control. That's just the way things are. No one's perfect. Straight people don't have the same problems as gay people, though.

Therapist: What kind of problems do straight people have?

Elliot: They don't have to worry about being ridiculed, taunted, rejected and laughed at all the time. People wouldn't be pushing my buttons all the time.

Therapist: Really? What about a straight person who is obese? How about a straight person who is covered in planters warts? How about a straight person with two heads?

Elliot: That's an extreme example, but I see what you're saying.

Therapist: I don't think it's a matter of being straight or gay. I think it's what you think about being gay and what you are telling yourself about yourself. When you think about being ridiculed, what are you telling yourself?

Elliot: When my dad ridiculed me, I thought, 'You don't care about me and I can't stand that.'

Therapist: Anything else?

Elliot: It's funny, but it was like I was looking for him to forgive me for being gay. I said I was looking for acceptance, but I was really looking for forgiveness. I was sort of saying, 'I know this is bad and that I am not perfect, but I want you to forgive me for turning out this way.'

***

Session Six

Therapist: What do you tell yourself about being gay? I mean, if someone said, '*Elliot*, you are a big *faggot*,' what would you tell yourself?

Elliot: I don't know.

Therapist: Close your eyes and pay attention to your thoughts. Listen to your self-talk. What are you saying to yourself about that statement?

Elliot: I don't like it. That's for sure.

Therapist: What about it don't you like?

Elliot: My God, where do I begin?

Therapist: Listen for words like *should, ought, must, have to* and *need*. Look for self-talk that contains those words. Just say whatever comes to your mind.

Elliot: People shouldn't talk to me that way. People should be more courteous. I should be less obvious and not appear to be gay. I should learn to act straight. I thought I had, but I must not be doing a good job. If I act gay, I am a piece of shit. If I act straight I am good. It's my fault that people are making fun of me. Acting gay is bad. If people know I'm gay that means I am not like other people and that is really bad. If someone calls me a *faggot*, I will have to stand up for myself and fight them. I really don't want to fight people. But if I don't fight them, that makes me a *faggot*. I don't want to be a *faggot* or fight. So I am just standing there. I'm not fighting and I am not running. But I look like a coward and a *faggot* and there's nothing I can do about it.

Therapist: That's a lot to think about.

Elliot: You asked for it.

Therapist: Yes, I did.

Elliot: I never have just listened to my own thoughts, but I am surprised at what I am thinking about. To be honest with you, I think a lot of the fear I have of being viewed as a gay person is that people will confront me and I will have to do something back to them. That really is my big problem. Of course I still think I am a piece of shit anyway. But my biggest problem is that I feel like I have to do something if people make fun of me. I am not really a good fighter. If I say something back, it might cause a fight. It's pretty much a problem with standing up for myself. If I didn't think people would fight me, it would be a different thing altogether.

Therapist: Is that your only option? Fight or be a coward?

Elliot: I suppose:

Therapist: Could you do anything else?

Elliot: You can always do something else.

Therapist: What thoughts would you have to give up, to do something differently – something that you would be happy with doing? If you had one wish that would help handle this situation, what would it be?

Elliot: That they would burst into flames?

Therapist: That's one option. How about something that is more related to you and your thinking.

Elliot: I'm not sure what to do. That's why I came here. This is sort of the same thing my dad did. He didn't say I was a *faggot*, but he might as well have.

***

Session Seven

Therapist: Can you ever be just one thing?

Elliot: I guess not.

Therapist: You may very well be a combination of a lot of things – both good and not so good.

Elliot: Yes, that's true.

Therapist: It's one thing to say it's true. It's another thing to believe that it's true.

Elliot: I understand – sort of.

Therapist: It looks to me like if someone insults you, you make yourself entirely bad. Like when your father rejected you and you became a piece of shit. You all of a sudden became unacceptable. Then our imaginary person called you a *faggot*, and you became that thing. It's like there is a magic wand that makes you bad. Is there one that makes you good?

Elliot: Yeah, when people praise me. Then I think I'm good.

Therapist: Until someone tells you you're not?

Elliot: Yes.

Therapist: You may want to get hold of that. From where I'm sitting, it seems like it would be very exhausting.

Elliot: What do you suggest?

Therapist: I would suggest that you, first, begin to realize that you are neither good nor bad. You are a number of things, unequal in value and significance. You are too many things to be called by just one name. You can begin to view the things people say to you, both good and not so good, as suggestions. No more than suggestions.

Elliot: So, if someone tells me I am a no good, stinking rotten person - that is a suggestion?

Therapist: Of course. And it is a suggestion you can either accept or reject. Simply because someone believes this about you is not proof enough that it's true. If someone doesn't like you, is that enough evidence that you are unlikeable? It would be insane for you to believe it anyway. There is overwhelming evidence that it isn't true. It would be insanity to give this statement much more than that - an insane suggestion from a person who appears to have a very little grasp on reality.

Elliot: It's like they're crazy and they are ranting about crazy shit.

Therapist: That's another way of looking at it. And if you join in with it, you are acting insanely by accepting their insane reality.

***

Session Eight

Elliot: It's sort of like arguing with a crazy person.

Therapist: Yes, and would you want to fight a crazy person for saying crazy things to you?

Elliot: No. I would probably feel sorry for them.

Therapist: Let's use that same imagery to understand your father's response to you when you told him you are gay. Is there any connection you can make?

Elliot: My father isn't crazy. He is pretty sane, actually.

Therapist: Great! But was he saying some crazy stuff to you?

Elliot: Yes. He was saying that gay people are filthy, an abomination, disgusting, drug addicts, sex fiends and pedophiles.

Therapist: And what is sane about that?

Elliot: Nothing . . . unless I think it's sane to think that.

Therapist: Is it sane to think you are an abomination filthy, drug addicted, disgusting pedophile?

Elliot: It's pretty insane for someone to think that. I still don't like it.

Therapist: I'm glad you don't like it. I wouldn't expect you to like it.

Elliot: Well, how do I get rid of my anger?

Therapist: You can change your thoughts.

Elliot: Like thinking what he's saying is insane?

Therapist: How would you respond to an insane person who said these things to you?

Elliot: I get it.

Therapist: Good, but how would you respond? What would you tell yourself?

Elliot: I would tell myself that he doesn't know how to behave. He is hallucinating about something. He is saying things that are crazy and he can't help it.

Therapist: What emotion would you feel then?

Elliot: I guess I would feel sad. Maybe I would think it was funny.

Therapist: Shame on you.

Elliot: Is that a suggestion?

Therapist: Very funny.

***

Session Nine

Therapist: We're coming to the end of our session. This is where I like to get some feedback, just to make sure we are on the same page. Tell me what we talked about today. Or, better yet, tell me what you remember most about our session.

Elliot: Most? I think when you said, 'You cannot have happiness in your life unless you are loved and respected by everyone you meet?'

Therapist: What about that interests you?

Elliot: Sometimes I think I cannot be as happy as I'd like to be unless people appreciate me and respect me. Like it's the end of the world if someone doesn't like me. I just wish I could do more about that.

Therapist: It isn't easy, but you can.

Elliot: If you could help me with that, I would really appreciate it.

Therapist: What do you tell yourself, say, when someone thinks you behaved badly?

Elliot: Tell myself?

Therapist: Yes, listen to your mind. It will tell you your beliefs. It will tell you what you think of certain things. Let's say someone treated you rudely, say at the convenient store. Say the cashier talked on her cell phone and didn't treat you very well, as a customer. What would you tell yourself about that?

Elliot: I would tell myself she was rude.

Therapist: And . . . ?

141

Elliot: She shouldn't be?

Therapist: And . . . ?

Elliot: She should change.

Therapist: Why?

Elliot: Because I want her to?

Therapist: What if she doesn't change?

Elliot: She would be a horrible person and I couldn't stand that.

Therapist: So you couldn't live happily while she was in the world acting rudely?

Elliot: Now I get it.

Therapist: If your happiness depends on how well people cooperate with your wishes, you are likely to be unhappy a lot of the time.

Elliot: I get that part, but what can I do instead.

Therapist: Remember how we talked about viewing the situation differently?

Elliot: About seeing people who act strangely as insane?

Therapist: Sure. If the cashier were viewed as crazy, what kind of behavior would you expect from her?

Elliot: Crazy?

Therapist: Should crazy people act any differently?

Elliot: I guess not.

Therapist: Put that in your own words.

Elliot: I can still be happy in my life, even if people are acting crazy and saying crazy things. I don't have to fight anyone or yell back at them. I can think, 'Boy, this person is really making a lot of poor choices. They are saying all sorts of crazy shit and behaving strangely. I think I should just move away from them.'

Therapist: What about your thoughts concerning being gay?

Elliot: I guess I still feel like it would be better to be straight.

Therapist: Can you be happy in your life if you're not like other people?

Elliot: Sure I can. I just have to stop thinking that just because someone thinks something bad about me that it's true. I have to give myself my own value, rather than taking everyone's random suggestions of my value. I am in charge of the way I feel because I am in charge of the way I think. If I think differently, I will feel differently. I will never like it that people don't like me because I'm gay, or any other reason. But I certainly can live my life and be happy. Yes, I think I can do that.

SANDY'S CASE STUDY

Therapist: How can I help you?

Sandy: I hate being fat.

Therapist: How is being fat a problem for you?

Sandy: Nobody likes fat people. I am always afraid that someone will make fun of me in public.

Therapist: Is there anything else about being fat that you don't like?

Sandy: I hate pretending all the time that I am happy being fat.

Therapist: Anything else?

Sandy: I just hate having to lie all the time and pretend people don't notice how fat I am.

Therapist: OK . . . anything else?

Sandy: That's about it. I want to be different. I don't want to be this way.

Therapist: Any of these things more important to you than any other?

Sandy: I guess that everyone hates fat people.

Therapist: Wow! That's really terrible. How do you know that everyone hates fat people?

Sandy: Because I'm fat and I know. I live through it every day.

Therapist: Do I hate you?

Sandy: I don't know. Do you?

Therapist: No.

Sandy: How do I know that?

Therapist: You'll just have to take my word for it.

Sandy: I'm lost.

Therapist: Yes, let's re-focus. I'm wondering if people generally liked fat people, how you would feel about that.

Sandy: I would be a lot happier.

Therapist: Would you want to be fat then?

Sandy: Yes. I wouldn't have any problems then.

Therapist: Would everyone like you then?

Sandy: I guess not. Someone wouldn't like me for some other reason.

Therapist: I don't think we are talking about you being fat at all.

Sandy: What are we talking about?

Therapist: Maybe we are talking about how well you accommodate not being liked.

Sandy: Maybe, but I can change myself if people don't like me for other reasons. I mean if people don't like what I'm wearing or what I'm driving, I can change it. I can't change being fat. At least it wouldn't be very easy to do. It would take a lot of *something* I don't have. I don't want to lose weight. I just want to be liked for who I am.

Therapist: So if I didn't like your shirt, you would change it?

Sandy: I wouldn't change it, but I wouldn't wear it here again.

Therapist: What would it mean if I didn't like your shirt?

Sandy: I guess it means you don't like me.

Therapist: What if I didn't like you?

Sandy: I would feel like I was bad.

Therapist: Simply because I didn't like your shirt?

Sandy: I guess.

Therapist: Again, I don't think we're talking about you being fat at all.

Sandy: Goodness. What are we talking about now?

Therapist: We are talking about you and how much you dislike yourself for any reason anyone can hand to you. We can actually do something about that. Do you want to do something about that?

Sandy: I never really looked at it like that.

Therapist: What would it mean if someone told you they didn't like you because you were fat?

Sandy: It would mean I couldn't make them like me right away.

Therapist: And what would it mean to you not to be able to make someone like you right away?

Sandy: I guess I would feel . . . like . . . powerless. Like I would be really off balance until they saw past my fat and liked me.

Therapist: Is it true that if someone didn't like you because you are fat that you are entirely bad?

Sandy: To them I would be.

Therapist: That may be. Is it true that you are entirely bad because someone doesn't like your shirt? Your car? Your weight?

Sandy: Not really. I mean it isn't true unless I think it's true.

Therapist: How do you know it's not true?

Sandy: Because they might not like me, but I have some friends who like me and don't care that I'm fat.

Therapist: I thought you said EVERYONE hates fat people.

Sandy: I guess I was exaggerating.

Therapist: It may not be such a good idea to exaggerate when you're in emotional turmoil.

Sandy: True.

Therapist: So what's so special about the person we are talking about? The one who doesn't like you?

Sandy: I guess I want everyone to like me.

Therapist: Is it your goal to have everyone like you?

Sandy: I guess.

Therapist: We may want to work on that goal.

STRATEGY TWENTY SEVEN

I can plan my own behavior

We've discussed the idea that people have a tendency to externalize the source of their emotions and expect emotional and behavioral change from others – rarely from themselves. We've also talked about how people have the tendency to make negative and critical WHOLE evaluations of others who do not cooperate with our expectations. When we are not getting what we want, we might think: *You should greet me when I come into your store. You didn't and that makes you a bad person. You should be kind and courteous when I place my food order. You weren't, so that makes you an asshole. You should thank me after I pay you. You didn't, so you are bad and should be fired and live a miserable and thankless existence.*

This level of evaluation is too critical and fuels the process of expressing anger, preventing the expression of more manageable, life-sustaining emotion. This method of emotional problem-solving also denies the existence of human imperfection. Essentially, if someone does something we don't like, they are entirely bad. When we apply the word *should* to behavior, we are expecting ourselves and others to meet a standard of perfection or ideal. And each time we impose an ideal standard on ourselves and others, and that standard isn't met, our memories of past experiences will likely interfere with our immediate emotional response.

***

Anger is often generated from focusing on the negative aspects of an experience and forming negative expectations of similar, future experiences. Very little in life works out perfectly or meets the ideal standard you set for it. If we expect perfection, we will often be disappointed. Each time that standard is not met, instead of expecting it to happen again we can resolve the problem by hoping and planning for a better future experience.

Self-talk can create an expectancy of something negative.

My client, the one with the counter-people-problems, decided to do something about it. He was tired of being angry. He chose to practice on the counter person at his physician's office. He imagined that the counter woman would not greet him, as she normally didn't. Even worse, she would call him by his first name (something he abhorred and considered disrespectful) and ask him questions about his personal medical condition by shouting them across the waiting area. His first step was to change his self-talk: *I cannot predict who will assist me at the counter. I can plan my own behavior. Instead of going in telling myself she will be rude, I could go in telling myself I won't be angry if she does, instead. I will tell myself that she is emotionally handicapped. I can't be mad at a handicapped woman. I can be the person I want others to be!*

***

Self-talk is the language we use to communicate with ourselves about everything within our perception. Self talk is part of our thinking process made into behavior. As we are presented with problems, or decisions, we draw on our familiarity with them and tell ourselves how we solved the problem in the past. Negative self-talk prevents us from rationally, effectively solving our problems.

Self talk is often repetitive, words and phrases we grow accustomed to telling ourselves. They can be positive or negative. They are often automatic and are not the result of any real analysis or problem-solving. They are essentially our knee-jerk reaction. We don't often search for evidence that contradicts our self-talk. Improving one's emotional intelligence requires that specific activity.

***

Changing our self-talk is a time-consuming task, requiring a lot of effort and cognitive vigilance. Even those who have spent a lifetime trying to establish a fact-based process for improving emotional intelligence often cling to some of their old, faulty beliefs. Ideally, peoples' beliefs should evolve as they gain new experiences. But that isn't always the case. You have to keep in mind that you spent your entire life building the beliefs you now hold. Dismantling them will not be a simple task.

***

What does it mean to give up an established belief for a new idea? Simply, no NEW idea will ever be accepted without first wresting, to some degree, with an already-established belief. And established beliefs often prevail, even when the beliefs act against our own self-interest.

***

Beliefs, for example, are our personal laws, our expectations of others. Our worldview. Our beliefs guide our decision-making and give us a sense of justice. To increase our emotional intelligence, however, we must break our own internal laws and discover new ideas, establish more flexible beliefs. Straddling the chasm between your current beliefs and entertaining new ones will present your biggest challenge to improving your emotional intelligence.

It will take the force of will to accomplish.

STRATEGY TWENTY EIGHT

She pissed me off

Beliefs are often confused with facts. It is this confusion that often interferes with our internal logic. If we believe something is a fact, we will behave as if it were. Anger, rage, hatred, resentment, loathing and revulsion are all examples of emotions that are derived from beliefs confused with fact.

***

Thinking, believing and emoting are all interrelated, joined to one another so inextricably that it is often quite difficult to tell them apart.

***

Emotion is a product of thought. The particular thought that produces an emotion is a belief: *I believe that people should always behave courteously. That person is not behaving courteously. I am angry because I believe they should behave differently and they are not.*

***

Often our beliefs are entrenched in how we believe we *should, ought, must, have to* and *need* to be treated by others.

Thinking about beliefs creates emotion.

Our society teaches us very early in life that the source of our emotions is external of us – that it comes from others: *She won't share her toys with me. She makes me mad. I think I will pull her hair, to make her cooperate with me.*

We also learn early in life to describe the source of our unhappiness in terms of *how other people make us feel.*

***

I began my own journey toward understanding the source of my emotions that weekend in Chicago with Al. He asked me to describe the source of my anger. Previous to my contact with him, not only had no one ever asked me to locate the source of my emotions, but it never occurred to me to even think that my emotions were impulses produced almost entirely by me. I responded by saying my emotions were just there, like berries on a bush, fungus on a rock, sand on the beach. They weren't exactly physical things: *They are Instinct. They come from my gut – from my heart – somewhere below my head.*

That question was answered more accurately upon my second session at the student counseling center. My original therapist had resigned, dropping out of her doctoral program to return to Michigan to manufacture and sell wind chimes. I said to my new therapist, "I am really angry when people steer their cars at me when I'm jogging. They *make* me so mad."

"What do you mean *they make you mad?*" He continued to pet his cat.

"Well, when I go jogging, people seem to get a kick out of scaring me to death by steering their cars at me. They flick their cigarettes out the window at me."

"How is that a problem for you?"

"How is it a problem for me? They shouldn't do that. It makes me mad! People should behave better than that! They should follow the law."

"Do you need people to follow the rules of driving in order to be happy in your life?"

"It would be nice."

"Sure it would. It would be nice to be the king of the %$#&^ world, too. But do you NEED people to drive according to the accepted in order to be happy in your life? If you do, you and traffic are headed for a very unhappy life together."

"No, I guess I don't NEED it to be that way to be happy in my life."

"Then stop telling yourself you NEED it. PREFER it over how people are actually behaving. WANT it. Be sad when you don't get it. Anything but NEEDING it! Tell yourself you can live in a world where people act foolishly from time to time. Change your belief in what you think you need to something you're more likely to get. And go jogging on the track behind the gym. Are you *$%$*ing nuts!? You're gonna get yourself killed!"

***

Suffice it to say, when you have an emotion, you THINK first. The thought is often fleeting, but it is a thought, nonetheless. More specifically, it is a thought related to a belief you hold. The belief I held in how people should behave, in order for me to be happy in my life, was actually interfering with my happiness: *If people don't drive according to the laws, I will be unhappy until they do. I will be consumed with hatred and I will be unhappy all the time. That will show them!* This belief actually prevented me from making decisions about my safety.

***

My belief was a fleeting thought, and I had to learn to capture it. Not with a butterfly net, but with a rusty, old bear trap. I had to get hold of it and take it apart with my teeth and bare knuckles. Of course it would be nice if everyone followed the law and behaved according the rules. But they don't and they won't unless they feel like it. Instead of the belief: *People must follow the law in order for me to be happy. If they don't, I will be angry and they will be damned.* I could adopt a new belief: *People break the law and I am sad that they do. I can accept it. I won't be happy about it. I can be happy in my life, nonetheless.*

So, anger can become sadness, by changing thoughts and beliefs to those that are more manageable. But you have to capture your thought, your belief, first, in order to take control of it and make new sense of your world. Another example might be: *I believe that people must always be kind and considerate when they are interacting with me,* a common belief held by a great number of people. *(See if you can make a rational statement from that belief.)*

***

The emotion you have when interacting with others will depend on how closely others adhere to your personal beliefs (and you to theirs). If you're being treated kindly and considerately by others, your emotion could range from happiness to complacency. If you're not being treated kindly and considerately, your emotional reaction could range from anger to rage. How? Well, if you tell yourself: *In order to be happy, I MUST be treated kindly and considerately by people who interact with me,* you're likely to be angry when people don't share your belief in how they should interact with you. If you change your belief to: *I would like to be treated kindly and considerately, but it is not a necessity of my overall happiness if I'm not,* you will likely feel an emotion altogether different. It may be best, overall, not to make other people's behavior a condition of YOUR happiness.

It will take the force of will to do this.

STRATEGY TWENTY NINE

What if you were worthless?

Beliefs are like viruses. They influence nearly every emotion you have. We've discussed the idea that your beliefs guide your behaviors and can impact your physical and emotional health. Like a virus, beliefs can spread, bolstering the strength of your other beliefs. For example, your belief that you should receive respect from other people in order to be happy in your life may be related to your belief in your own self worth, "What would it mean if someone disrespected you?"

"Well, it would mean they think I am not worthy of respect."

"And if you are not worthy of respect, what would that mean?"

"It would mean I am worthless."

"And if you were worthless?"

"I would have no value as a person."

***

Your belief in your own self-worth may be related to your self-image, your very humanness! Like any virus, its potential for life depends on feeding it the right nutrients to keep it alive. Challenging irrational, unhealthy self-talk is like white blood cells attacking a virus, swooping in to destroy the belief and help you regain your emotional equilibrium and health. What would it mean to give up some of your beliefs?

It will take the force of will to find out.

STRATEGY THIRTY

Do you want to stop being nuts?

My third therapist, a psychologist, was in his late fifties, bald, casually dressed. Walking into his office was like waking up in the lower drawer of a dusty filing cabinet. There were books, magazines and yellowed paper scattered everywhere: "REBT, eh?" he responded to my question about my *preference*. "Have a seat." He moved a pile of newspapers off the seat of the chair, across from the couch he would sit in, leaving a half-eaten apple for me to toss by its withered stem into the wastebasket, "Here, sit." A Brussels griffon jumped into my seat and began licking its paws. I looked at the therapist and, ever so faintly, smiled, "Just shoo him off. Shoo," he said. He fanned his yellow legal pad at him. The Brussels jumped down and ran behind the gray, metal desk, "How can I help you?" He looked at his watch, "Two-thirty."

"I am a student and I have to do 10, I mean 8 hours of therapy as a client." I reached out my therapy log for him to initial, "I wanted to work some more with someone who knows REBT."

He took the tattered therapy log and tossed it onto his disordered desk, "OK, then. What's on your mind?"

"I'm bald."

"How is that a problem for you?"

"I look old?"

"What does it mean to you to look old?"

"It means I'm ugly." I paused, waiting for him to take exception with that assessment.

He didn't. He just trotted ahead, "And if you're viewed as old, what does that mean?"

"It means no one will think I am attractive."

"And if no one thinks you're attractive?"

"Well, no one will care about me."

"It's quite unlikely that would happen, but what would it mean if no one cared about you?"

"It would mean I don't deserve to be loved. It would mean I was unlovable."

Suddenly he slammed his hands on the arms of his tattered chair, "All of this from being bald? Are you nuts?"

"I guess," I said, actually interested in what had just happened.

"Well, at least we can agree on one thing. He leaned in toward me. Do you want to stop being nuts?"

In essence, he was saying that my emotional reaction to going bald did not come from how other people felt about it. My emotional reaction came from what I believed about it, from my perception of myself and how much value I placed on opinion. My emotional reaction to my impending baldness had little to do with my baldness. In order to retain my value as a human being, I was telling myself I NEEDED the approval of others. I had to have a full head of hair, and then people would like me, and only then I would be loveable.

"What would it mean if no one cared about you?"

"Nothing. I really don't care about what people think about me."

"Really? So if someone didn't like you, you wouldn't care at all?"

"I guess I would care."

"True, you would care. You care about everything TO SOME EXTENT. We just have to help you care to a lesser extent."

Amazingly, he told me that if I continued to depend on other people for my personal value, if a miracle occurred and I actually grew a full head of hair (or get some from the Hair Club for Men) I would still not be suitable for anyone's affection, "People might complain about your eye color, your education, your weight, your breath, the shape of your ass. You would NEVER be satisfied." The Brussels jumped into his lap and he petted its caramel-colored fur. I cupped my hand over my mouth and blew into it, trying to smell my own breath, "It will all end when you understand that you can have value as a human being without hair. Hell, you could lose both of your ears and still retain your intrinsic human value."

All of a sudden, I was back in Chicago with Al. My emotions come FROM me. There was no escaping it. They come from how I VIEW how people interact with me; how they speak to me; how they behave toward me. MY INTERPRETATION of what they do, what they say is the thing that causes me to feel an emotion: *In order to feel an emotion, I first have to think. I have to think about what is happening and I have to interpret it. I have to apply a meaning to it.*

That message took me by surprise, AGAIN!

Only this time it was an Ah-ha! moment.

STRATEGY THIRTY ONE

Are you trying to trick me?

When you are asked to give up a belief, say, your belief in how people should treat you, you are being asked to give up a part of yourself. Many of your beliefs are warnings, personal messages, morals and ideas conveyed to you by someone you respected or something you experienced that proved important to you. Think of one belief you hold that doesn't work especially well.

Give it up!

Sacrifice it!

If you are hesitating, join the club. People can be counted on to hold on to and defend their beliefs until they have some other belief, something better with which to replace it. You cannot simply point out the errors in your thinking. You must also accept that your belief is harmful and willingly replace it with a new belief. It's like trying to replace a bad habit with a good one.

Takes time.

***

Everyone knows cigarette smoking is dangerous, but until a suitable alternative is developed to replace smoking cigarettes, something acceptable to that individual smoker, they will continue to smoke. (The one exception I have found is the smoking patch. It works well if you glue it directly over the smoker's mouth.)

The same goes for beliefs.

Until you can replace your operational belief, the notion you use to make judgments, with a more suitable alternative, one you're willing to accept, you will hold on to the bad habit. For example, "Is it true that no one will ever love you again, now that your girlfriend dumped you?"

"Looks that way."

"If no one ever loves you again, what will that mean?"

"It would mean that my girlfriend was right about me. I deserve to be alone."

"If you were alone, what would that mean?"

"It would mean that I wasn't loveable."

"What does it mean to not be lovable?"

"It means I am not worthy of anyone's love."

"Do you really think that you are unworthy of anyone's love, because your girlfriend broke up with you?"

"Sort of."

"Were you lovable before you had your former girlfriend?"

"Yeah, I had a girlfriend before this last one. She loved me, so I guess I was lovable."

"So now you are entirely unlovable because you got dumped by your girlfriend?"

"I see where you're going."

"Can you be loveable and be single?"

"I guess so."

"What do you have to do to change your feeling about being alone?"

"Change my belief about what it means."

***

It has been suggested that less demanding, more flexible beliefs can help increase emotional intelligence. The development of a belief may include any number of contributions from a large number of sources. A single belief can be composed of past experiences, your grandmother's hopes, world disasters, social customs you picked up and adopted as your own. If this is true and your beliefs are a collection of experiences, before you would be willing to give up a belief, you would have to weigh the consequences against the benefits. It's as if I were offering you $50,000.00 for your '62 Plymouth Valiant. You would be intrigued, interested and highly motivated. You know you would be better off if you made the trade, but you would still want to know more. You would hold on to your car until you understood the offer, fully. *Are there any strings attached? Are you trying to trick me? Are you crazy?*

***

Flexibility in your beliefs may help you achieve a higher emotional competency. In addition, emotional intelligence can be cultivated if you work forcefully, persuasively and vigorously against your tendency to think irrationally, using a system of logical, pragmatic evaluation of thought in relation to the noxious events that occur in your life.

"So you actually can live with being disrespected?"

"Sure I can. I wouldn't be at all happy about it, but I could live happily."

"But would you be angry?"

"Yes, but not as much."

"How would you reduce the anger you would feel?"

"I would change my belief. I would remind myself that people act foolishly sometimes and I can still live and be content with my own life, when they do."

***

People seem to instinctively hold on to what they already know, if to give up a belief means that they will be left with a belief they don't accept. In the case of the '62 Plymouth Valiant, the concern may be a matter of overall well-being: *Will what I have to endure by selling this car outweigh the cost? Am I being hoodwinked? Is my car somehow more valuable than I thought? Will I be hurt by this deal?* The surrendering of beliefs is reasoned in much the same way. The decisions to give up what you already believe, what you depend upon to get through each day, includes issues of psychological safety, protection and wellbeing. Exchanging one belief for another seemingly exposes an individual to vulnerability. Even the slightest threat to one's psychological safety can be perceived as a threat to the individual's very existence. You will have to have a new belief, one you can trust and count on for safety, to replace the one you are forfeiting.

***

Our daily lives are often filled with a number of challenges to our emotional state. In that frame of mind, it may seem impossible to exchange one belief for another. After all, when you are in survival mode and your rational mind is disengaged, it is unlikely that you will be considering emotional options.

***

Practice, before the emotional trauma erupts, is the best way to prepare. Your consciousness is focused on fear, not reasoning. It is impractical to even try to make clear choices when your mind and body are responding to threat. In a state of anger and rage, the long-term consequences of your choices are not important to you. It is best, then, to address your dysfunctional beliefs, before you have to draw on them for support.

It will take the force of will to do that.

STRATEGY THIRTY TWO

Articulated Thought

Most often, when people experience psychological hardship, they find themselves trying to solve their emotional problems inside their own head. Thinking, endlessly reviewing the same information, looping into the same emotionally charged result, never really resolving anything. Just like using thought only to find a solution to a complicated math problem, trying to solve a complicated emotional problem within the confines of your own mind may be just as elusive. Staying focused is often a challenge, and complex problems are better understood by drawing on our total competencies.

***

People seem to prefer to use spoken words over thoughts, alone. Words bring emotion to life. So, if you're lucky, you may find someone who is willing to listen. Most of us prefer to consciously articulate our thoughts. When we tell and retell the problem from the perspective we experienced it, there seems to be more possibility for understanding. Not to mention the support and sympathy we get, when others tell us how horribly we've been treated. Speaking out loud often helps to add clarity to the problem, maintain our focus, expand our ability to reason and better understand our issues and problems.

***

Most of us are at a loss when we find there is no one to talk with about what is concerning us. When something happens that disrupts our emotional stability, our balance, we might call a friend, a family member or, if things are really out of control, we might make an appointment with a therapist. While we wait for the return phone call, we sit and think, summoning the problem to mind, rolling it over and over in our own minds, and waiting for someone to reach out to us.

To talk.

Something you might think of doing to increase your emotional intelligence is to change who you turn to for help. Add a new dimension to your thinking and behaving. It's time to become an active part of your own emotional life.

***

We don't ordinarily think about ourselves as a mental health resource, when we have a problem. As a matter of fact, discussing your emotional issues with yourself would probably rank last in the list of potential collaborators, rivaling the discussions we have with our dogs. After all, isn't talking to oneself is a sign of mental illness? We allow ourselves the comfort of speaking to ourselves when we want to remember a series of numbers, the directions to the main road or a list of items we need from the grocery store. We sing to the radio, and hope no one hears us making up the words. We can have elaborate discussions with our deceased relatives, but we can never experience ourselves in that same manner. Somehow we learn that we must keep an emotional distance from ourselves.

We seem to be in contempt of our own guidance.

167

In order to achieve the highest benefit from this program, it's time to start depending on yourself and your own best advice. Risk is a good thing in behavior change. Nothing changes without some level of risk. You have to take risk in order to escape the status quo. After all, it is your embrace of the status quo that has prevented you from achieving improved emotional intelligence.

Begin a relationship with yourself by saying out loud: *Hello! I have been with you my entire life* and *I have never once introduced myself to you. I am pleased to know you* and *I can't wait to share my thoughts* and *ideas with you. We know each other pretty well, already. Just by sharing experiences. You are really the only one I can truly trust* and *who knows me. Let's make a plan to talk every day. Maybe on the way home from work, in the car. That way we can be alone,* and *we won't have to think about anything else.*

Listen to your own voice.

Talk to yourself about the ABCs.

Learn how to dispute out loud.

Learn the voice of your teacher.

The voice of your true best friend.

It will take the force of will to do that.

Do your homework!

That little girl from my elementary school just may have been responsible for me spending much of my academic life trying to understand the substance of emotion. I write this book with her smile fixed in mind. She could withstand my misdirected wrath and keep on smiling.

This book offers no magical elixirs or ethereal philosophy that will resolve your issues with your mother or overeating or tell you why people treat you badly. It does contain good, practical solutions and easy-to-learn methods that, if you choose, will bring about immense change in your life. You will learn skills that will come in handy if you find yourself relapsing – reverting back to your old ways of thinking and behaving.

People, who are treated for emotional concerns, after a period of wellness, think they are cured for life. Consequently, when they slip back into old habits, and discover their old problems are still present to some degree, they are likely to despair and give up working on themselves altogether. Oftentimes, when relapse is likely, people will return to therapy. This book, however, promotes not only self-efficacy, but also a new way of living.

I believe that people are better prepared for life when they learn to take greater responsibility for their own personal growth and change. Not when they develop a dependency on pills and therapists to help resolve their emotional issues. So, you will be expected to practice your new-found skills independently for the rest of your life!

***

At times, the statements I've made and the solutions I have suggested may be hard to incorporate into your daily life. After all, you have been living your life a certain way using your own thinking and reasoning skills for, well, your whole life. Changing the way you think, behave and, ultimately, live your life will take a great deal of courage and strength. You will have to commit to that goal.

***

I carried that little girl's note in my backpack, untouched, until lunch. When the bell rang, I took off across the ball field. The dugout was the most private place I could find. The note was folded into some sort of box shape, and I was careful not to tear it, treating it as if it were a map to a secret pirate treasure. I finally got it unraveled and I remember smirking at her good penmanship. The note said: *Do your homework.* She had drawn little smiley faces into each of the Os.

Of course, we were in love from that point on. We never spoke a word to each other, but each time I turned in my homework, and each time it was returned with a passing grade, I looked at her and she at me and we both smiled. Life changed for me after that. I was paroled from Murder's Row and allowed to roam among the living.

The rest is history.

So, for the little girl at South Elementary School, this book promotes the use of homework as a vital part of the process of improving emotional intelligence. Your homework should consist of one or more self-directed activities, designed to encourage you to independently act against how you traditionally respond to adversity. Your homework should result in some level of change to your thoughts and behaviors. For instance, if you fear a certain social activity, you might intentionally place yourself in the feared social situation. While immersed in the activity, you will be ready to address your thoughts in relation to that situation. That way, you will be aware, in real-time, of what you tell yourself, how you thwart your own ambitions and how to work through them.

I can only say that the suggestions I have made to help increase your emotional intelligence will work if you let them. I cannot promise you that there will never come a time in your emotional life that you won't ever feel miserable again, no matter how much you take away from your reading. On the contrary, you will feel every single emotion you ever felt before reading this book. Only now you will celebrate anger, sadness, irritability, resentment and annoyance. You will view these as opportunities for learning, rather than setbacks.

With practice and patience you can develop alternatives methods for overcoming emotional hardship by reaching an emotional resolution that suits your personal goal of happiness and, of course, by sucking a lemon and tasting cinnamon.

It will take the force of will to do that.

BIBLIOGRAPHY

Abrams, M & Abrams, L.: A Brief Biography of Dr. Albert Ellis 1913–2007

Antonakis, J. (2009). "Emotional intelligence": What does it measure and does it matter for leadership? In G. B. Graen (Ed). LMX leadership--Game-Changing Designs: Research-Based Tools (Vol. VII) (pp. 163-192). Greenwich, CT: Information Age Publishing. Download article: http://www.infoagepub.com/products/Predators-Game-Changing-Designs

Antonakis, J., & Dietz, J. (2011a). Looking for Validity or Testing It? The Perils of Stepwise Regression, Extreme-Scores Analysis, Heteroscedasticity, and Measurement Error. Personality and Individual Differences, 50(3), 409-415, http://dx.doi.org/10.1016/j.paid.2010.09.014

Antonakis, J., & Dietz, J. (2011b). More on Testing for Validity Instead of Looking for It. Personality and Individual Differences, 50(3), 418-421, http://dx.doi.org/10.1016/j.paid.2010.10.008

Antonakis, J.; Ashkanasy, N. M.; Dasborough, M. (2009). "Does leadership need emotional intelligence?". The Leadership Quarterly 20 (2): 247–261. doi:10.1016/j.leaqua.2009.01.006.

Austin, E.J. (2008). A reaction time study of responses to trait and ability emotional intelligence test items. Personality and Individual Differences, 36, 1855-1864.

Bar-On, Reuven; Parker, James DA (2000). The Handbook of Emotional Intelligence: Theory, Development, Assessment, and Application at Home, School, and in the Workplace. San Francisco, California: Jossey-Bass. ISBN 0787949841. pp. 40-59

Bar-On, R. (1997). The Emotional Quotient Inventory (EQ-i): a test of emotional intelligence. Toronto: Multi-Health Systems.

Bar-On, R. (2006). The Bar-On model of emotional-social intelligence (ESI). Psicothema, 18 , supl., 13-25.

Boyatzis, R., Goleman, D., & Rhee, K. (2000). Clustering competence in emotional intelligence: insights from the emotional competence inventory (ECI). In R. Bar-On & J.D.A.

Bradberry, Travis and Greaves, Jean. (2009). Emotional Intelligence 2.0. San Francisco: Publishers Group West. ISBN 9780974320625

Brody, N. (2004). What cognitive intelligence is and what emotional intelligence is not. Psychological Inquiry, 15, 234-238.

Schulte, M. J., Ree, M. J., & Carretta, T. R. (2004). Emotional intelligence: Not much more than g and personality. Personality and Individual Differences, 37, 1059–1068, http://dx.doi.org/10.1016/j.paid.2003.11.014

Cornwall, M. (2008). Using articulated thought disputation (ATD) to strengthen rational emotive behavior theory (REBT). Northcentral University, 2008 ISBN 0549611142, 9780549611141.

Cote, S. and Miners, C.T.H. (2006). "Emotional intelligence, cognitive intelligence and job performance", Administrative Science Quarterly, 51(1), pp1-28. Retrieved from http://en.wikipedia.org/w/index.php?title=Emotional_intelligence&oldid=455756959

Ellis, A. & Abrams, M. (2008). Personality Theories: Critical Perspectives.   Thousand Oaks, Ca.:Sage Publications.

Ellis, A. (1964) if this be heresy... Is pornography harmful to children? In The Realist No.47 pp.17-8, 23

Ellis A. (2000). Can rational emotive behavior therapy (REBT) be effectively used with people who have devout beliefs in God and religion?. Professional Psychology: Research and Practice, 31(1), Feb 2000. pp. 29–33

Eysenck, H.J. (2000). Intelligence: A New Look. ISBN 0765807076

Locke, E.A. (2005). "Why emotional intelligence is an invalid concept". Journal of Organizational Behavior 26 (4): 425–431. doi:10.1002/job.318.

Farley, F. (2009). Albert Ellis (1913–2007). American Psychologist, Vol 64(3), pp. 215–216

Fiori, M., & Antonakis, J. (2011). The ability model of emotional intelligence: Searching for valid measures. Personality and Individual Differences, 50(3), 329-334, http://dx.doi.org/10.1016/j.paid.2010.10.010

Gardner, H. (1983). Frames of mind. New York: Basic Books.

Gardner, J. K.; Qualter, P. (2010). "Concurrent and incremental validity of three trait emotional intelligence measures". Australian Journal of Psychology 62: 5–12. doi:10.1080/00049530903312857.

Goleman, D. (1998). Working with emotional intelligence. New York: Bantam Books Hans, T. (2000). A meta-analysis of the effects of adventure programming on locus of control. Journal of Contemporary Psychotherapy, 30(1),33-60.

Harms, P. D.; Credé, M. (2010). "Remaining Issues in Emotional Intelligence Research: Construct Overlap, Method Artifacts, and Lack of Incremental Validity". Industrial and Organizational Psychology: Perspectives on Science and Practice 3 (2): 154–158. doi:10.1111/j.1754-9434.2010.01217.x.

Harms, P. D.; Credé, M. (2010). "Emotional Intelligence and Transformational and Transactional Leadership: A Meta-

Analysis". Journal of Leadership & Organizational Studies 17 (1): 5–17. doi:10.1177/1548051809350894. http://digitalcommons.unl.edu/cgi/viewcontent.cgi?article=1013&context=leadershipfacpub.

Hattie, J. A., Marsh, H. W., Neill, J. T. & Richards, G. E. (1997). Adventure Education and Outward Bound: Out-of-class experiences that have a lasting effect. Review of Educational Research, 67, 43-87.

Kluemper, D.H. (2008) Trait emotional intelligence: The impact of core-self evaluations and social desirability. Personality and Individual Differences, 44(6), 1402-1412.

Korzybski A. (1933). Science and Sanity. Institute of General Semantics, 1994, ISBN 0-937298-01-8

Landy, F.J. (2005). Some historical and scientific issues related to research on emotional intelligence. Journal of Organizational Behavior, 26, 411-424.

Leuner, B. (1966). Emotional intelligence and emancipation. Praxis der Kinderpsychologie und Kinderpsychiatrie, 15, 193-203.

Mamlin, N., Harris, K. R., Case, L. P. (2001). A Methodological Analysis of Research on Locus of Control and Learning Disabilities: Rethinking a Common Assumption. Journal of Special Education, Winter.

Marsh, H. W. & Richards, G. E. (1986). The Rotter Locus of Control Scale: The comparison of alternative response formats and implications for reliability, validity and dimensionality. Journal of Research in Personality, 20, 509-558.

Marsh, H. W. & Richards, G. E. (1987). The multidimensionality of the

Rotter I-E Scale and its higher order structure: An application of confirmatory factor analysis. Multivariate Behavioral Research, 22, 39-69.

Martins, A.; Ramalho, N.; Morin, E. (2010). "A comprehensive meta-analysis of the relationship between emotional intelligence and health". Journal of Personality and Individual Differences 49 (6): 554–564. doi:10.1016/j.paid.2010.05.029.

Mattiuzzi, P.G. Emotional Intelligence? I'm not feeling it. everydaypsychology.com

Mayer, J.D., Salovey, P., Caruso, D.R., & Sitarenios, G. (2003). Measuring emotional intelligence with the MSCEIT V2.0. Emotion, 97-105. http://www.psykologi.uio.no/studier/drpsych/disputaser/folles dal_summary.html Hallvard Føllesdal - 'Emotional Intelligence as Ability: Assessing the Construct Validity of Scores from the Mayer-Salovey-Caruso Emotional Intelligence Test (MSCEIT)' PhD Thesis and accompanying papers, University of Oslo 2008

Mayer, J.D., Salovey, P., Caruso, D.L., & Sitarenios, G. (2001). Emotional intelligence as a standard intelligence. Emotion, 1, 232-242.

Mayer, J.D., & Salovey, P. (1997). What is emotional intelligence? In P. Salovey & D. Sluyter (Eds.), Emotional development and emotional intelligence: Implications for educators (pp. 3-31). New York: Basic Books.

Mikolajczak, M., Luminet, O., Leroy, C., & Roy, E. (2007). Psychometric properties of the Trait Emotional Intelligence Questionnaire. Journal of Personality Assessment, 88, 338-353.

Mikolajczak, Luminet, Leroy, and Roy (2007). Psychometric Properties of the Trait Emotional Intelligence Questionnaire: Factor Structure, Reliability, Construct, and Incremental Validity in a French-Speaking Population. Journal of Personality Assessment, 88(3), 338–353

Nielsen, Stevan Lars & Ellis, Albert. (1994). A discussion with Albert Ellis: Reason, emotion and religion, Journal of Psychology and Christianity, 13(4), Win 1994. pp. 327–341

Palovey, P., & Mayer, J.D. (1990). Emotional intelligence. Imagination, Cognition, and Personality, 9, 185-211.

Parker, JDA; Taylor, GJ; Bagby, RM (2001). "The Relationship Between Emotional Intelligence and Alexithymia". Personality and Individual Differences 30: 107–115. doi:10.1016/S0191-8869(00)00014-3.

Payne, W.L. (1983/1986). A study of emotion: developing emotional intelligence; self integration; relating to fear, pain and desire. Dissertation Abstracts International, 47, p. 203A (University microfilms No. AAC 8605928)

Petrides, K.V. & Furnham, A. (2000a). On the dimensional structure of emotional intelligence. Personality and Individual Differences, 29, 313-320

Petrides, K.V., Pita, R., Kokkinaki, F. (2007). The location of trait emotional intelligence in personality factor space. British Journal of Psychology, 98, 273-289.

Petrides, K.V. & Furnham, A. (2001). Trait emotional intelligence: Psychometric investigation with reference to established trait taxonomies. European Journal of Personality, 15, 425-448

Pérez, J.C., Petrides, K.V., & Furnham, A. (2005). Measuring trait emotional intelligence. In R. Schulze and R.D. Roberts (Eds.), International Handbook of Emotional Intelligence (pp.181-201). Cambridge, MA: Hogrefe & Huber.

Petrides, K.V., & Furnham, A. (2003). Trait emotional intelligence: behavioral validation in two studies of emotion recognition and reactivity to mood induction. European Journal of Personality, 17, 39–75

Prospect Magazine: Albert Ellis. August 1, 2007 Issue 137 Jules Evans New York Times: Albert Ellis, Influential Psychotherapist, Dies at 93 psychotherapy.net: An Interview with Albert Ellis, PhD Rational Emotive Behavioral Therapy

Roberts, R.D., Zeidner, M., & Matthews, G. (2001). Does emotional intelligence meet traditional standards for an intelligence? Some new data and conclusions. Emotion, 1, 196–231

Rotter, J. (1966). Generalized expectancies for internal versus external control of reinforcements. Psychological Monographs, 80, Whole No. 609.

Salovey P and Grewal D (2005) The Science of Emotional Intelligence. Current directions in psychological science, Volume 14 -6 Bradberry, T. and Su, L. (2003). Ability-versus skill-based assessment of emotional intelligence, Psicothema, Vol. 18, supl., pp. 59-66.

Smith, M.K. (2002) "Howard Gardner and multiple intelligences", The Encyclopedia of Informal Education, downloaded from http://www.infed.org/thinkers/gardner.htm on October 31, 2005.

Smith, L., Ciarrochi, J., & Heaven, P. C. L., (2008). The stability and change of trait emotional intelligence, conflict communication patterns, and relationship satisfaction: A one-year longitudinal study. Personality and Individual Differences, 45, 738-743.

Thorndike, R.K. (1920). "Intelligence and Its Uses", Harper's Magazine 140, 227-335.

Taylor, Graeme J; Bagby, R. Michael and Parker, James DA (1997). Disorders of Affect Regulation: Alexithymia in Medical and Psychiatric Illness. Cambridge: Cambridge University Press. ISBN 052145610X. pp. 28-31

William Knaus, Jon Geis, Ed Garcia. A Message in Support of Dr. Albert Ellis from Three Former Directors of Training of the Albert Ellis Institute

Vernon, P.A.; Petrides, K.V.; Bratko, D.; Schermer, J.A. (2008). "A behavioral genetic study of trait emotional intelligence". Emotion 8 (5): 635–642. doi:10.1037/a0013439. PMID 18837613.

Vorst, HCM; Bermond, B (2001). "Validity and reliability of the Bermond-Vorst Alexithymia Questionnaire". Personality and Individual Differences 30 (3): 413–434. doi:10.1016/S0191-8869(00)00033-7.

Yankura J. & Dryden W. (1994). Albert Ellis. SAGE. Recollection of Stevan Lars Nielsen, Ph.D. who was present at the 90th birthday party The New Yorker: The Human Condition – Ageless, Guiltless NY Courts: Ellis v Broder (2006 NY Slip Op 26023) *References specific to Articulated Thought and Social Problem Solving*

Aguilar, N. (1997). Counseling the learner with chronic illness: Strategies for thehealthcare provider. *Journal of American Academy of Nurse Practitioners. 9*(4), 171-5.

Anderson, J. (2002). Executive coaching and REBT: Some

comments from the field. *Journal of Rational - Emotive & Cognitive -
Behavior Therapy, 20*(3-4), 223. Retrieved July 30, 2007, from
ProQuest Psychology Journals
database. (Document ID: 386245661).

Aristotle (350 BC). The nicomachean ethics. Retrieved May, 12,
2006, from
http://www.ilt.columbia.edu/publicATIONS/artistotle.html

Aviv, R. (2005). The interpretation of reams. Retrieved
September 12, 2006 from
http://www.villagevoice.com/people/0534,interview,67068,24.ht
ml

Beck, A. (1994). Foreword. In Kingdon & Turkington (Eds.),
Cognitive-behavioral therapy of schizophrenia (pp. v-vii). New
York: Guilford Press.

Berger, V. (2005). Rational emotive behavior therapy. Retrieved
August 10, 2007, from
http://www.psychologistanywhereanytime.com/treatment_and_t
herapy_psychologist/psychologist_rational_emotive_behavioral_t
herapy.htm

Bernard, M., & Wolfe, J. (2000). The RET resource book for
practitioners. New York: Institute for Rational-Emotive Therapy.

Berne, J. (2004). Think-aloud protocol and adult learners. *Adult
Basic Education, 14*(3), 153-173.

Besser, A., Flett, G., & Hewitt, P. (2004). Perfectionism,   cognition, and
affect in response to performance failure to success. *Journal of
Rational-Emotive & Cognitive Behavior Therapy, 22*(4).

Biggam F., & Power K. (1999). Social Problem Solving skills
and psychological distress among incarcerated young offenders:
The issue of bullying and

victimisation. *Cognitive Therapy and Research, 23*, 307-326.

Bishop, W., & Fish J. (1999). Questions as interventions: Perceptions of Socratic, solution focused, and diagnostic questioning styles. *Journal of Rational-Emotive and Cognitive-Behavior Therapy, 17*(2), 115-140.

Blankstein, K., & Winkworth, G. (2004). Dimensions of perfectionism and levels of attributions for grades: Relations with dysphoria and academic performance. *Journal of Rational-Emotive & Cognitive Behavior Therapy, 22*(4).

Boelen, P., & Baars, L. (2004). Two studies on the psychometric properties of the belief scale. *Gedragstherapie, 37*(4).

Boelen, P., Kip, H., & Voorsluijs, J. (2004). Irrational beliefs and basic assumptions in bereaved university students: A comparison study. *Journal of Rational-Emotive & Cognitive Behavior Therapy, 22*(2).

Bransford, J., & Stein, B. (1984). The IDEAL problem solver. New York: W. H. Freeman.

Broder, M. (2001). Dr. Albert Ellis – Ellis in his own words – On success. *Journal of Rational – Emotive & Cognitive - Behavior Therapy, 19*(2), 77. Retrieved September 6, 2006, from ProQuest Psychology Journals database. (Document ID: 386235861).

Broder, M. (2000). Making optimal use of homework to enhance your therapeutic effectiveness. *Journal of Rational Emotive and Cognitive Behavior Therapy, 8*(1), 3-18.

Byrne, J. (2006). Research issues in coaching, counseling, and psychotherapy. Some ideas and developments. Retrieved February 12, 2006, from http://rebt.cc/_wsn/page12.html

Chang, E., D'Zurilla, T., & Sanna, L. (2004). Social Problem

Solving: theory, research, and training. APA: Washington, D.C.

Chang, E., D'Zurilla, T., & Maydeu-Olivares, A. (1994). Assessing the dimensionality of optimism and pessimism using a multimeasure approach. *Cognitive Therapy and Research, 18*, 143-160.

Clark, D. (1999). Constructivism. Retrieved September 15, 2007, from http://www.nwlink.com/~donclark/hrd/history/history.html

Collins, A., Brown, J., & Newman, S. (1989). Cognitive apprenticeship: Teaching the crafts of reading, writing, and mathematics. In L. B. Resnick (Ed.). Knowing, learning and instruction: Essays in honor of Robert Glaser (pp. 453-494). Hillsdale, NJ: Lawrence Erlbaum Associates.

Corsini, R., & Wedding, D. (1995). Current Psychotherapies. Itasca, Illinois: F.E. Peacock Publishers.

Criddle, W. (2007). The transition from therapist to executive coach. *Journal of Rational-Emotive & Cognitive-Behavior Therapy (25)*2, 121-141.

D'Zurilla, T., Nezu, A., & Maydeu-Olivares, A. (2002). Social Problem Solving Inventory-Revised (Social Problem Solving – R). North Tonawanda, NY: Multi-Health Systems, Inc.

D'Zurilla, T., & Nezu, A. (1999). Problem Solving therapy: A social competence approach to clinical intervention (2nd ed.). New York: Springer.

D'Zurilla, T., & Maydeu-Olivares, A. (1995). Conceptual and methodological issues in Social Problem Solving assessment. *Behavior Therapy, 26*, 409-432.

D'Zurilla, T. J. (1986). Problem Solving therapy: A social

competence approach to clinical intervention. New York: Springer Publishing Co.

D'Zurilla, T. J., & Nezu, A. (1982). Social Problem Solving in adults. In P. C. Kendall (Ed.), Advances in cognitive-behavioral research and therapy. New York: Academic Press.

D'Zurilla, T., & Godfried, M. (1971). Problem Solving and behavior modification. *Journal of Abnormal Psychology, 78*, 107-26.

David, D. and Avellino, M. (2002) A Synopsis of REBT Research: Basic/Fundemental and Applied Research. Retrieved February 11, 2006, from http://rebt.cc/db5/00479/rebt.cc/_download/ASYNOPSISOF RebtRESEARCH.doc

David, D., Macavei, B., & Szentagotai, A. (2005). Cognitive restructuring and mental contamination: An empirical re-conceptualization. *Journal of Rational-Emotive & Cognitive-Behavior Therapy, 23*, 1, 21-55.

David, D., Szentagotai, A., Eva, K., & Macavei, B. (2005). A synopsis of rational-emotive behavior therapy (REBT): Fundamental and applied research. *Journal of Rational – Emotive & Cognitive - Behavior Therapy, 23*(3), 175-221. Retrieved September 4, 2006, from ProQuest Psychology Journals database. (Document ID: 997217251).

Davidson, G., Vogel, R., & Coffman, S. (1997). Think-aloud approaches to cognitive assessment and articulated thoughts in simulated situations paradigm. *Journal of Consulting and Clinical Psychology, 65*(6), 950-958.

Davison, G., Robins, C., & Johnson, M. (1983). Articulated

thoughts during simulated situations: A paradigm for studying cognition in emotion and behavior. *Cognitive Therapy and Research,* 7, 17-40.

DiLiberto, L., Katz, R., Beauchamp, K., & Howells, G. (2002). Using articulated thoughts in simulated situations to assess cognitive activity in aggressive and nonaggressive adolescents. *Journal of Child and Family Studies, 11,*(2), 179-189.

Dryden, W. (2007). My idiosyncratic practice of REBT. Retrieved May, 4, 2007 from, http://www.psychotherapy.ro/index2.php?option=com_content &do_pdf=1&id=30

Dryden, W. (2005). Rational emotive behavior therapy. In: Comparative treatments for borderline personality disorder. Freeman, A., Stone, M. & Martin, D. (2005) New York: Springer Publishing Co.

Dryden, W., & Neenan, M. (2003). The REBT therapist's pocket companion. Retrieved January 4, 2007, from http://www.walden3.org/Pocket%20REBT%204%20Therapists. pdf

Dryden, W., Ferguson, J., & Clark, T. (1989). Beliefs and inferences: A test of rational-emotive hypothesis 1. Performing in an academic seminar. Journal of Rational-Emotive and Cognitive-Behavior Therapy, 7, 119– 129.

Du Plessis, M., Möller, A., & Steel, H. (2004). The Irrational Beliefs Inventory: Cross-cultural comparisons between South African and previously published Dutch and American samples. *Psychological Reports, 95*(3, Part1). (Document ID: 386245621).

Dyer, W. (1977). Erroneous Zones. New York: Avon.

Eckhardt, C., & Jamison, T. (2002). Articulated thoughts of male
     perpetrators of dating violence during anger arousal.
     Cognitive Therapy and Research,
     26, 289-308.

Eckhardt, C., Barbour, K., & Davison, G. (1998). Articulated
     irrational thoughts in maritally violent and nonviolent men during
     anger arousal. *Journal of*
     Consulting and Clinical Psychology, 66, 259-269.

Ellis, A. (2003a). Early theories and practices of rational emotive
     behavior therapy and how they have been augmented and revised
     during the last three decades. *Journal of Rational - Emotive &*
     Cognitive - Behavior Therapy: Albert Ellis' 90th Birthday Celebration: His
     Contribution, 21. Retrieved September 9, 2006, from, ProQuest
     Psychology Journals database. (Document ID: 424411351).

Ellis, A. (2003b). The relationship of rational emotive behavior
     therapy (REBT) to Social Psychology. *Journal of Rational - Emotive*
     & Cognitive - Behavior
     Therapy, 21(1), 5. Retrieved September 2, 2006, from ProQuest
     Psychology Journals database. (Document ID: 440142431).

Ellis, A. (2003c). Early theories and practices of rational emotive
     behavior theory and how they have been augmented and revised
     during the last three decades. *Journal of Rational-Emotive &*
     Cognitive-Behavior Therapy,
     21(3/4).

Ellis, A., & Joffe, D. (2002). A study of volunteer learners who
     experienced live sessions of rational emotive behavior therapy in
     front of a public audience. *Journal of Rational - Emotive & Cognitive -*
     Behavior Therapy, 20(2), 151.

Retrieved September 2, 2006, from ProQuest database. (Document ID: 386235871).

Ellis, A. (2001). Feeling better, getting better, staying better. New York: Impact Publishers, 2001. ISBN 1-886230-35-8.

Ellis, A. (2001). Reasons why rational emotive behavior therapy is relatively neglected in the professional and scientific literature: *Journal of Rational-Emotive and Cognitive-Behavior Therapy, 19*(1), 67-74.

Ellis, A., & Grieger, R. (1997). Handbook of Rational-Emotive Therapy. New York: Springer Publishing Co.

Ellis, A., & Harper, R. (1997). A guide to rational living (3rd ed.). Hollywood, CA: Wilshire.

Ellis, A. (1995). Changing rational-emotive therapy (RET) to rational emotive behavior therapy (REBT). *Journal of Rational-Emotive & Cognitive-Behavior Therapy, 3*(2).

Ellis, A., & Dryden, W. (1987). The practice of rational-emotive therapy. New York: Springer.

Ellis, A. (1950). An introduction to the principles of scientific psychoanalysis. *Genetic Psychology Monographs, 41.*

Ellis, A., Eisenbud, J. Pederson-Krag, G. & Fodor, N. (1947). Telepathy and psychoanalysis: A critique of recent "findings". *Journal Psychiatric Quarterly, 21*(4), 607-631.

Ellis, A., & Conrad, H. (1946). The validity of personality questionnaires. *Psychological Bulletin, 43.*

Emerson, R. (1841). Self reliance. Retrieved September 5, 2007, from http://www.smartwomeninvest.com/emerson.pdf

Engels, G., Garnefski, N., & Diekstra, R. (1993). Efficacy of rational-emotive therapy: A quantitative analysis. *Journal*

of Consulting and Clinical Psychology, 61(6), 1083. Retrieved
September 4, 2006, from PsycARTICLES database. (Document
ID: 293526571).

Fenichel, M. (2000). Asynchronously live from APA 2000.
Retrieved September 2, 2006 from
http://www.fenichel.com/Beck-Ellis.shtml

Flanagan, R., Povall, L., Dellino, M., & Byrne, L. (1998). A
comparison of problem solving with and without rational
emotive behavior therapy to improve children's social skills.
*Journal of Rational-Emotive & Cognitive-
Behavior Therapy, 16*(2), 125-134.

Friedberg, R., Miller, R., Perymon, A., Bottoms, J., & Aatre, G.
(2004). Using a session feedback form in cognitive
therapy with children. *Journal of Rational - Emotive
& Cognitive - Behavior Therapy, 22*(3), 219-230. Retrieved August
27, 2007, from ProQuest Psychology Journals database.
(Document ID: 817362381).

Froggart, W. (2005). Rational emotive behaviour therapy.
Retrieved September 3, 2006, from
http://www.rational.org.nz/prof/docs/Intro-
REBT.pdf#search=%22rebt%20biopsychosocial%22

Froggatt, Wayne (2005). A brief introduction to rational emotive
behaviour therapy. 3rd Edition, New Zealand: Centre for
Cognitive Behaviour Therapy.

Gateley, G. (1999). Rational-behavior therapy as correcting
demamaps. *et Cetera, 56*(3), 274-279. Retrieved January 24, 2007,
from Research Library database. (Document ID: 46562130).

Glaser, N., Kazantzis, N., Deane, F., & Oades, L. (2000). Critical
issues in using homework assignments within cognitive

behavioural therapy for schizophrenia. *Journal of National-Emotive and Cognitive-Behavior Therapy.* *18*(4), 247-261.

Gonzalez, J., Nelson, J., & Gutkin, T. (2005). Rational emotive therapy with children and adolescents: A meta-analysis. *Journal of Emotional & Behavioral Disorders, 12*(4).

Gazzaniga, M. (2006) Leon Festinger. Lunch with Leon. *Perspectives on Psychological Science 1* (1), 88–94.

Gossette, R., & O'Brien, R. (1993). Efficacy of rational emotive therapy (RET) with children: A critical reappraisal. *Journal of Behavior Therapy and Experimental Psychology, 24*, 15-25.

Greeno, J. (1997). On claims that answer the wrong questions. *Educational Researcher, 26*(1), 5-17.

Guterman, J., & Rudes, J. (2005). A solution-focused approach to rational-emotive behavior therapy: toward a theoretical integration. *Journal of Rational – Emotive & Cognitive - Behavior Therapy, 23*(3), 223-244. Retrieved August 27, 2007, from ProQuest Psychology Journals database. (Document ID: 997217241).

Haaga, D., & Davison, G. (1993). An appraisal of rational-emotive therapy. *Journal of Consulting and Clinical Psychology, 61*, 215-220.

Haaga, D., & Davison, G. (1989). Slow progress in rational-emotive therapy outcome research: Etiology and treatment. *Cognitive Therapy and Research, 13*, 493-508.

Haaga, D., & Stewart, B. (1992). Self-efficacy for recovery from a lapse after smoking cessation. *Journal of Consulting and Clinical Psychology, 60*, 24-28.

Halasz, G. (2004) In conversation with Dr Albert Ellis.

Australasian Psychiatry, 12(4).

Hauck, P. (2001). When Reason Is Not Enough. *Journal of Rational-Emotive and Cognitive-Behavior Therapy, 19*(4), 245-257.

Heery, M. (2000). An interview with Albert Ellis, PhD. Retrieved August 5, 2006 from http://www.psychotherapy.net/interview/Albert_Ellis

Huitt, W. (1992). Problem Solving and decision making: Consideration of individual differences using the Myers-Briggs Type Indicator. *Journal of Psychological Type*, 24, 33-44.

Hurley, D. (2004). From therapy's Lenny Bruce: Get over it! Stop whining! Retrieved October 1, 2006 from, http://www.rebt.ws/recentarticles.html

Johnson, M., & Kazantzis, N. (2004). Cognitive behavioral therapy for chronic pain: Strategies for the successful use of homework assignments. *Journal of Rational-Emotive & Cognitive-Behaviour Therapy. 22*(3), 189-218.

Johnson, W. (2005). Rational emotive behavior therapy for disturbance about sexual orientation. In: Casebook for a spiritual strategy in counseling and psychotherapy.

Jones, R. (1968). A factorial measure of Ellis's irrational belief system. Unpublished doctoral dissertation.Texas Technological College .

Kahn, B., & Kahn, W. (2001). Is REBT marginalized? A survey of counselor educators. *Journal of Rational - Emotive & Cognitive - Behavior Therapy,19*(1), 5. Retrieved September 18, 2006, from ProQuest Psychology Journals database. (Document ID: 386235771).

Kanter, J. (1988). Clinical issues in the case management relationship. *New Directions for Mental Health Services,* 40, 15-27.

Kendall, P. (1984). Cognitive processes and procedures in
    behavior therapy. In T.G. Wilson, C.M. Franks, K.P. Brownell, &
    P.C. Kendall (eds.), Annual review of behavior
    therapy (pp. 123-164). New York: Guilford Press.

Keyes, K. (1997). Handbook to Higher Consciousness. Arrojo
    Rande: Love Line Books.

Kinney, A. (2000). The intellectual-insight problem: Implications
    for assessment and rational-emotive behavior therapy. *Journal of*
    Contemporary Psychotherapy, 30(3), 261. Retrieved January 11, 2007,
    from ProQuest
    Psychology Journals database. (Document ID: 386244251).

Kucan, L., & Beck, I. (1997). Thinking aloud and reading
    comprehension research:Inquiry, instruction, and social
    interaction. Review of Educational Research, 67,271–299.

Lodge, J., Tripp, G., & Harte, D. (2000). Think-aloud, thought-
    listing, and video-mediated recall procedures in assessment of
    children's self-talk. *Cognitive*
    Therapy and Research, 24(4), 399-418.

McCown, W., & Carlson, G. (2004). Narcissism, perfectionism
    and self-termination from treatment in outlearner cocaine users.
    Journal of Rational-Emotive & Cognitive Behavior Therapy, 22(4).

McDermut, J. F., Haaga, A. A. F., & Bilek, L. A. (1997).
    Cognitive bias and irrational beliefs in major depression
    and dysphoria. Cognitive Therapy and Research, 21,
    459–476.

Macavei, B. (2005). The role of irrational beliefs in the rational
    emotive behavior theory of depression. *Journal of Cognitive &*
    Behavioral Psychotherapies, 5(1).

Mahoney, M. (2004). What is constructivism and why is it

growing? *Contemporary Psychology, 49,* 360-363.

Marini, A., & Genereux, R. (1995). The challenge of teaching for transfer. In A. McKeough, J. Lupart, & A. Marini (Eds.), Teaching for transfer: Fostering generalization in learning (pp. 1-19). Mahwah, NJ: Lawrence Erlbaum Associates.

Martin-Hanson, L. & Johnson, J. (2006). Think-aloud in inquiry science. *Scienceand Children, 44*(1), 56-59.

Mulhauser, G. (2007). An introduction to rational emotive behavior therapy. Retrieved January 3, 2007, from http://counsellingresource.com/types/rational-emotive/index.html

Neenan, M. (2001). REBT 45 Years on: Still on the sidelines. *Journal of Rational – Emotive & Cognitive - Behavior Therapy, 19*(1), 31. Retrieved September 18, 2006, from ProQuest Psychology Journals database. (Document ID: 386235751).

Neenan, M. (1999). Problem-creating to Problem Solving. Retrieved March 3, 2006, from http://www.isma.org.uk/stressnw/problems.htm

Nielsen, S. (2004). A Mormon rational emotive behavior therapist attempts qur'anic rational emotive behavior therapy. In: Casebook for a spiritual strategy in counseling and psychotherapy. Richards, P. (2004). Dept of Counseling Psychology & Special Education, Brigham Young University. Washington, DC: American Psychological Association.

Overholser, J. (2003). Rational-emotive behavior therapy: An interview withAlbert Ellis. *Journal of Contemporary Psychotherapy, 33*(3), 187.Retrieved September 2, 2006, from ProQuest Psychology Journals database. (Document ID: 348759781).

Palmer, S. (1997). A rational emotive behavior approach to
hypnosis. The Rational Emotive Behavior Therapist, 5, 1, 34-54.

Pedersen, S., & Liu, M. (2003). The transfer of Problem Solving
skills from a problem-based learning environment: The effect of
modeling an expert's cognitive processes. *Journal on Technology in
Education, 35*(2), 303-320.

Pedersen, S., & Liu, M. (2002). The transfer of Problem Solving
skills from a problem-based learning environment: The
effect of modeling an expert's cognitive processes. *Journal of
Research on Technology in Education
35*(2), 303-320.

Polya, G. (1971). How to solve it. Princeton, NJ: Princeton
University Press.Popa, S. (2001). Interview with Albert
Ellis: The "cognitive revolution" inpsychotherapy.
Romanian Journal of Cognitive and Behavioural Psycho   therapies, 1, 7-
17.

Rayburn, N., & Davison, G. (2002). Articulated thoughts about
antigay hate crimes. *Journal Cognitive Therapy and
Research, 26*(4), 431-447. Reinhard, J. (2000).
Limitations of mental health case management: A rational
emotive and cognitive therapy perspective. *Journal of
Rational - Emotive & Cognitive – Behavior Therapy, 18*(2), 103.
Retrieved August 27, 2007, from ProQuest
Psychology Journals database. (Document ID: 386235821).

Robb, H., Backx, W., & Thomas, J. (1999). The use of cognitive,
emotive and behavioral interventions in rational emotive behavior
therapy when learners lack emotional insight. *Journal of Rational-
Emotive & Cognitive-behaviorTherapy,17*, 201-209.

Robertson, D. (2001). REBT, philosophy and philosophical

counseling. Retrieved June 22, 2006, from http://www.practical-philosophy.org.uk/Volume3Articles/REBT.htm

Rorer, L. (1999). Dealing with the intellectual-insight problem in cognitive and rational emotive behavior therapy. *Journal of Rational - Emotive & Cognitive - Behavior Therapy, 17*(4), 217. Retrieved January 5, 2007, from ProQuest Psychology Journals database. (Document ID: 337476351).

Salsbery, K. (2005). [Review of the book Rational Emotive Behavior Therapy: It Works for Me -- It Can Work for You]. Retrieved November 7, 2006, from http://mentalhelp.net/poc/view_doc.php?id=2711&type=book&cn=91

Savron, G., Bartolucci, G. & Pitti, A. (2004). Psychopathological modification after cognitive behaviour treatment of obsessive-compulsive learners. *Rivista di Psichiatria, 39*(3).

Schuster, S. (1999). Philosophical counseling and rationality. Retrieved June 2, 2007, from http://www.geocities.com/centersophon/press/ox99.html

Smith, M., Glass, G., & Miller, T. (1980). The benefits of psychotherapy. Baltimore: Johns Hopkins University Press.

Smith, M., & Glass, G. (1977). Meta-analysis of psychotherapy outcome studies. American Psychologist, 32,752-760.

Solomon, A., Bruce, A., Gotlib, I. H., & Wind, B. (2003). Individualized measurement of irrational beliefs in remitted depressives. Journal of Clinical Psychology, 59, 439–455.

Still, A., & Dryden, W. (2003). Ellis and Epictetus: Dialogue to method inpsychotherapy. *Journal of Rational - Emotive & Cognitive - BehaviorTherapy, 21*(1), 37. Retrieved September 2, 2006, from ProQuest Psychology Journals database. (Document ID: 440142401).

Still, A. (2001). Marginalisation is not unbearable. Is it even undesirable? *Journal of Rational - Emotive & Cognitive – Behavior Therapy, 19*(1), 55. Retrieved October 1, 2006, from ProQuest Psychology Journals database. (Document ID: 386245561).

Terjesen, M., DiGiuseppe, R., & Gruner, P. (2000). A review of REBT research in alcohol abuse treatment. *Journal of Rational - Emotive & Cognitive - Behavior Therapy: Cognitive-Behavioral Treatment of Addictions, Part I, 18*(3), 165. Retrieved September 18, 2006, from ProQuest Psychology Journals database. (Document ID: 386235661).

Tiba, A. (2005). Demanding brain: Between should and shouldn't. *Journal of Cognitive & Behavioral sychotherapies, 5*(1).

Trower, P., & Jones, J. (2001). How REBT can be less disturbing and remarkably more influential in Britain: A review of views of practitioners and researchers. *Journal of Rational-Emotive & Cognitive-Behavior Therapy, 19*(1), 21-30.

Twerell, T. (1999). Presentation and defense of the use of cognitive behavioral therapy as seen in rational emotive behavioral therapy as a pastoral counseling tool http://www.nyccc.org/nyccc008.htm

Walen, S. DiGiuseppe, R. & Dryden, W. (1992). A practitioner's guide to rational-emotive therapy. New York: Springer.

Zettle, R., & Hayes, S. (1980). Conceptual and empirical status of rational-emotive therapy. *Progress in Behavior Modification, 9*, 125-166.

Ziegler, D. (2003). The concept of psychological health in rational emotive behavior therapy. *Journal of Rational-Emotive & Cognitive-Behaviour Therapy. 21*(1), 21-36.

Ziegler, D. (1999). The construct of personality in rational emotive behaviour therapy (REBT). *Journal of Rational-Emotive & Cognitive-Behaviour Therapy. 17*(1), 19-32.

Made in the USA
Lexington, KY
08 September 2012